India

India

BY ERIN PEMBREY SWAN

Enchantment of the World
Second Series

Children's Press®

A Division of Scholastic Inc.

NEW YORK   TORONTO   LONDON   AUCKLAND   SYDNEY
MEXICO CITY   NEW DELHI   HONG KONG
DANBURY, CONNECTICUT

Frontispiece: Elephants and their handlers at a celebration in Jaipur

Consultant: Dr. Sumit Ganguly, professor of Asian Studies and Government,
the University of Texas at Austin

Please note: All statistics are as up-to-date as possible at the time of publication.

Book production by Herman Adler Design

Library of Congress Cataloging-in-Publication Data

Swan, Erin Pembrey.
India / by Erin Pembrey Swan.
p. cm. — (Enchantment of the world. Second series)
Includes bibliographical references and index.
ISBN 0-516-21121-8
1. India—Juvenile literature. 2. India—Civilization—Juvenile literature.
[1. India.] I. Title. II. Series.
DS421 .S93 2002
954—dc21   00-066039

Acknowledgments

Special thanks to Sara Swan Miller, Peter Graves, and Margreet Cornelius. This book is dedicated to all the people in India.

Contents

Cover photo:
Taj Mahal

CHAPTER

 ONE   Summer Days 8

 TWO   Mountains, Deserts, and Plains 14

 **THREE** Palm Trees to Peacocks 24

FOUR   From the Beginning 34

 FIVE   The World's Largest Democracy 56

SIX   Earning a Living 66

SEVEN Who Lives in India? 78

EIGHT Temples, Mosques, and Gurdwaras 90

 NINE   Music, Movies, and Sports 104

TEN   Daily Routines 116

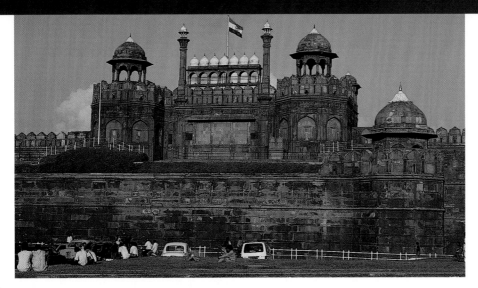
Red Fort

Timeline **128**

Fast Facts **130**

To Find Out More **134**

Index **136**

A Dravidian

CHAPTER ONE

Summer Days

I T IS DAWN ON THE HOT, DRY PLAINS OF UTTAR PRADESH. The sun has not come up yet, and the air is still cool. A young girl named Gita wakes up outside her family's hut and lies still for a moment, staring up at the slowly lightening sky. A rooster crows nearby, and Gita can hear the village cows begin to stir. Her brothers and sisters are still sleeping, huddled close together on a blanket spread on the ground. Her parents and grandparents sleep nearby on string beds called *charpoys*. It is May, the middle of the hot season, and the whole family must sleep outside to stay cool.

Opposite: **Village women drawing water from a well**

A woman shapes cow dung into patties to be used as fuel.

One by one, Gita's family begins to wake up. Everybody has a task to perform in the early morning. Gita's father lights the gas burner and boils milk to make the sweet, milky tea called *chai*. Her mother leans the charpoys against the wall of the hut and begins to sweep the dust in their yard into neat, crisscross patterns. Gita helps her brothers and sisters gather cow dung, which their mother will shape into patties and stick on the walls of the hut to dry. When the dung is dry, it makes excellent fuel, especially in an area where there are few trees to burn.

Doing laundry in the river

Village schoolchildren
studying outdoors

After family members have drunk their tea and eaten a breakfast of unleavened bread, they split up for the day. Gita's father and older brother trek to the fields that they tend for one of the village landowners. They receive part of the profit from the crops they harvest. Although it is not a lot of money, it is enough to support the family. Gita's mother and older sister, Maya, hoist bundles of dirty clothes onto their heads and walk down to the stream to wash them. They dunk the clothes in the stream, lather them with soap, and then beat them over and over with a wooden paddle until they are clean. Other women from the village join them to do their laundry, laugh, and exchange gossip.

Gita and her younger brother and sister attend the village school. They sit on benches outside, in the shade of a banyan tree. They learn to read and write Hindi, their own language, and English, which was introduced by the British. They learn the history of their country, beginning as far back as 2500 B.C. Their teacher tells them about all the kinds of people who live in India and how they came there. They learn how India, which they call *Bharat*,

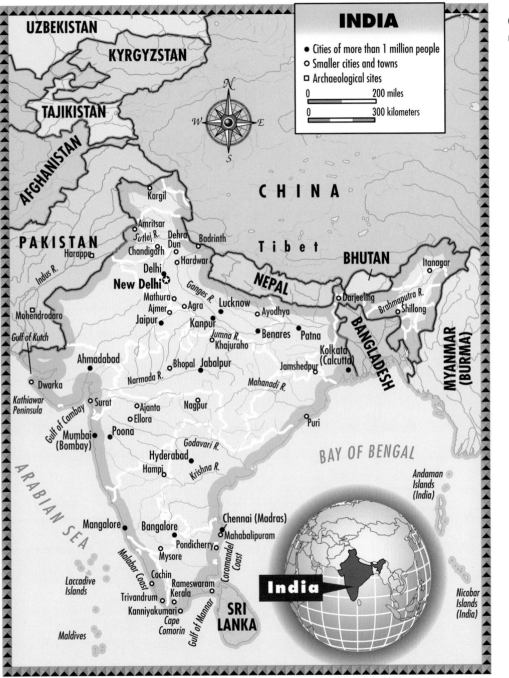

INDIA

- Cities of more than 1 million people
- Smaller cities and towns
- Archaeological sites

0 ——— 200 miles
0 ——— 300 kilometers

UZBEKISTAN

KYRGYZSTAN

TAJIKISTAN

AFGHANISTAN

PAKISTAN

CHINA

Tibet

BHUTAN

NEPAL

Itanagar

Kargil

Amritsar
Sutlej R. Dehra
Dun Badrinth
Chandigarh
Harappa
Hardwar
Delhi
New Delhi
Indus R.
Mathura
Ajmer Agra
Jaipur
Mohendrodaro
Gulf of Kutch
Ganges R. Lucknow
Ayodhya
Kanpur
Jumna R.
Khajuraho
Benares Patna
Darjeeling
Brahmaputra R.
Shillong
BANGLADESH
Kolkata
(Calcutta)

MYANMAR
(BURMA)

Ahmadabad
Dwarka
Kathiawar
Peninsula
Gulf of Cambay Surat
Mumbai
(Bombay)
Poona
Narmada R.
Ajanta
Ellora
Bhopal Jabalpur
Nagpur
Jamshedpur
Mahanadi R.
Puri

Hyderabad
Hampi
Godavari R.
Krishna R.

ARABIAN SEA

BAY OF BENGAL

Andaman
Islands
(India)

Mangalore Bangalore
Mysore
Pondicherry
Chennai (Madras)
Mahabalipuram
Coromandel Coast

Laccadive
Islands
Malabar Coast
Cochin
Trivandrum
Kanniyakumari
Cape
Comorin
Rameswaram
Kerala
Gulf of Mannar
SRI
LANKA

India

Maldives

Nicobar
Islands
(India)

gained its independence from Great Britain a little more than fifty years ago. Their teacher shows them a map of India and points to their location. Their state, Uttar Pradesh, lies in the north, in a stretch of land known as Hindustan. She tells them it is one of the most populated places in the whole world.

Gita knows that she lives in one of the largest and most important countries in the world. She knows that there are many kinds of people in India who practice many religions and speak many languages. She also knows that many people are like her and probably live similar lives.

Gita is a Hindu, and Hinduism is a religion that 80 percent of Indians practice. In the mornings, Gita watches her mother light incense and pray before the pictures of Hindu gods in their home. On special holidays, she goes with her mother to the village temple. They place offerings of food and flowers on the altar, asking the gods to bless their family with health and long life. These rituals are an important part of every Hindu household. Their religion tells Hindus how they should behave and dress, and even what they should eat. Gita, like most Hindus, is a vegetarian and thinks it is wrong to eat the flesh of animals. Some Hindus eat meat, but few will eat meat from cows, which are considered sacred animals.

After school, the children return home. The rest of the family is already there for the midday meal. Gita's mother has prepared a meal of steaming white rice, lentils, and boiled, spicy vegetables. They use the fingers of their right hands to eat. Afterward, they wash their hands and mouths with water that Gita's older sister has carried from the village well.

When the meal is over and the metal plates have been washed, they settle down for a short nap. Some of them curl up in the shade cast by the thatched roof of the hut. Others choose the comfortable canopy of a banyan tree. In the middle of the hot season, it is impossible to work during the midday hours. Instead, everyone rests and waits for the cool of evening before going back to work.

In a few hours, Gita's father and brother return to the fields, where they will work until sunset. Her mother and Maya gather with other women to shake the husks off rice, preparing it for cooking. Gita feels sorry for Maya, who is not allowed to play with them anymore. She is fifteen now and must help their mother instead. She is already wearing saris and brushing her hair with oil. Gita knows that her parents are looking for a husband for Maya. They have even hired a matchmaker to help them find one.

Water buffalo bathing

Gita is glad she is still a little girl. She races her younger brother and sister down to the stream, where they jump into the water. Other children join them to laugh and splash. Farther downstream, a man leads his herd of water buffalo in to bathe. The water buffalo look at the children curiously, but Gita doesn't notice. She is too busy splashing water on her little sister. They giggle and dunk each other under the water. All over India, other children are doing the same.

Mountains, Deserts, and Plains

I F YOU WERE TO TRAVEL THROUGH INDIA, YOU WOULD PASS
through almost every kind of landscape imaginable. In the
north are jagged mountain peaks and deep, rocky gorges. A
desert covers the northwest, but the coasts have palm trees and
cool sea breezes. Farther south are huge, flat plains that are
sometimes bare and dusty, and other times covered with rich,
fertile crops. Still farther south are mountains again, and eventually a wet, green land crissedcrossed by rivers and canals.

India is the seventh-largest country in the world. It
stretches about 2,000 miles (3,219 kilometers) from north to
south, and almost as much from east to west. It covers a total
of 1,269,438 square miles (3,287,590 sq km), forming a huge,
irregular triangle at the southern edge of Asia.

Often called a subcontinent because of its large size, India
shares its borders with six other countries. Bangladesh and
Myanmar (formerly Burma) lie to the east, and Nepal, Bhutan,

Opposite: **Rivers and canals
crisscross parts of Kerala.**

Mountains, Deserts, and Plains **15**

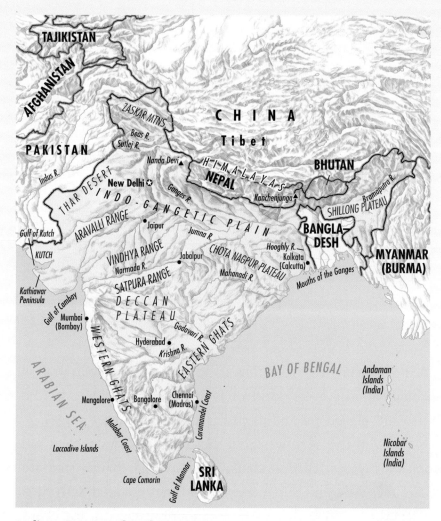

India's Geographical Features

Highest Elevation: Kanchenjunga Mountain, 28,208 feet (8,598 m) above sea level

Lowest Elevation: Trivandrum, in the state of Kerala, sea level

Longest River: Brahmaputra River, 1,880 miles (3,026 km) long

Highest Average Temperature: 113°F (45°C) in the far south

Lowest Average Temperature: −4°F (−20°C) in the far north

Greatest Annual Precipitation: 450 inches (1,143 cm) in Cherrapunji, in the state of Assam

Least Annual Precipitation: less than 10 inches (25 cm) in the Thar Desert

Coastline: 4,350 miles (7,001 km)

Greatest Distance North to South: approximately 2,000 miles (3,219 km)

Greatest Distance East to West: approximately 1,490 miles (2,398 km)

and Tibet (part of China) are directly north. Its neighbor in the northwest is Pakistan. The Arabian Sea laps against India's western coast, and the waters of the Bay of Bengal wash against the east. To the south lie the island nation of Sri Lanka (formerly Ceylon) and the huge, glittering expanse of the Indian Ocean.

The House of Snow

Rising up sharply from the Indian plains, the Himalaya Mountains stretch north to create the vast Tibetan plateau. *Himalaya* means "house of snow" in Sanskrit, India's ancient, classical language. The mountains reach east and west for 1,500 miles (2,414 km), forming three parallel ranges between

Kanchenjunga is India's highest mountain peak.

India and Tibet. The Himalaya are the highest mountains in the world, and the youngest. There are about 146 Himalayan peaks. Of these, 40 rise higher than 25,000 feet (7,620 meters). The Himalayan landscape ranges from tropical jungles in the foothills to snowy plateaus near Tibet. Three great rivers rise in the Himalaya— the Indus, the Ganges, and the Brahmaputra.

Rice fields planted on terraces cut into mountain slopes in Sikkim

People live throughout these mountains, planting their crops on terraces cut expertly into the slopes. Small roads and tiny footpaths twist over the hills, providing ways for people to get from place to place. When it rains, these roads often crumble into landslides, making traveling difficult. During the rainy season, it is common to see a bus or truck stopped short while the driver hauls fallen boulders out of the way so that the vehicle can move on.

The Indo-Gangetic Plain

Where the Himalaya flatten out, a whole different landscape begins. This is the Indo-Gangetic Plain, a flat area of land through which the Ganges River flows. This plain covers about 300,000 square miles (776,996 sq km) of northern

The Ganges River

Looking at India's Cities

Mumbai is India's largest city, with a population of about 15 million people. It was founded in 1661 by the British, who used technology to join its original seven islands into a single land mass. Mumbai quickly became India's most important trading port. Today it is known for its industries and fast-paced lifestyle. One favorite nighttime hangout is Chowpatty Beach, which

is thronged with food vendors, street performers, and pleasure-seekers after dark. At the southern end of Mumbai is the Gateway of India, built by the British in 1924 to welcome English ships to India. Mumbai used to be called Bombay, but its name was recently changed to celebrate its ancient Hindu heritage.

Kolkata is the nation's second-largest city. It houses about 12 million Hindus, Muslims, and Christians. The city was founded as a trading port by the British in 1686. It is now one of the most important cultural centers in India, famous for its painters, writers, and filmmakers. To celebrate its Indian history, its name was recently changed from Calcutta to Kolkata. Kolkata's crowds and pollution are relieved by the Maidan, a wide expanse of green parkland. The Howrah Bridge spans the Hugli River, connecting Kolkata with nearby Howrah. It is the busiest bridge in the entire world, with a daily crossing of about 60,000 vehicles and countless pedestrians.

With a population of about 6 million, Chennai (formerly Madras) is the largest city in southern India. Once a small fishing village on the Bay of Bengal, it became a major trading port when the British settled the East India Company there in 1639. Now a modern, bustling city with numerous textile mills and chemical plants, Chennai exports everything from leather goods and raw cotton to peanuts. It is also the center of the Tamil film industry and the host of the annual Carnatic Music and Dance Festival. Some of Chennai's famous landmarks include the University of Madras, the High Court Building, the Government Museum, and Fort St. George, built by the British in 1653.

India. Watered by the Indus, the Ganges, and the Brahmaputra Rivers, the Indo-Gangetic Plain has some of the most fertile soil in India. Many people make their homes there, where growing crops is made easier by the rich soil deposited by the rivers. In fact, the Indo-Gangetic Plain is one of the most densely populated areas in the world.

The Thar Desert

To the west of the Indo-Gangetic Plain lies the Thar Desert. This parched, sandy region covers about 100,394 square miles (260,019 sq km).

The Thar Desert receives less than 10 inches (25 centimeters) of rain a year. As in many deserts, camels are the common form of transportation because they can survive for a long time with only a little water. For many desert dwellers, a camel is a very precious possession.

Forested mountains of the Western Ghats

The Southern Peninsula

The Vindhya Range separates northern India from southern India. These mountains are about 4,000 feet (1,219 m) high, not nearly as tall as the Himalaya. Together with two other mountain ranges, the Eastern Ghats and the Western Ghats, the Vindhya Range forms the triangular Deccan Plateau.

Farming is more difficult on this plateau than it is on the northern plains. The dry season is longer, and the rainy season does not bring as much rain. Farmers on the Deccan Plateau must irrigate their land to grow crops.

The southern coasts are much more fertile because of the Godavari, the Krishna, and the Cauvery (or Kaveri) Rivers, which flow down from the hills. The Eastern and Western Ghats both smooth out along the coasts, giving way to wet, tropical land. The southwestern state of Kerala is probably the most tropical. Many rivers and canals crisscross the area nearest the sea, forming a region of sparkling backwaters and overhanging palm trees. As you might imagine, fishing is the main way of life here.

Hogenakal Falls on the Cauvery River

A Land of Extremes

India's climate, like its landscape, ranges from one extreme to another. In only a few hours, you can travel from the hot, sticky streets of Kolkata to the cold, rainy reaches of Darjeeling in the Himalayan foothills. Within a month, a parched, scorching plain can easily be flooded a few feet deep in rain.

India has three seasons—cool, hot, and wet. The cool season is India's winter and lasts from November to the end of January. Although the south remains relatively warm, the north can get fairly chilly, especially at night. During these months, the streets in the north are crowded with people wrapped in long shawls and blankets to keep warm. High in the Himalaya, it is snowy as well as cold.

Winters are cold in Ladakh, high in the Himalaya Mountains.

The hot season begins in February or March and usually lasts into June. This is a dry period of intense heat, with temperatures often rising above 104° Fahrenheit (40° Celcius). Because the plains become so unbearably hot, many people escape to the cool foothills of the Himalayas if they have the time and money to do so.

What Is a Monsoon?

The word *monsoon* comes from the Arabic word *mauism*, which means "season." A monsoon is a wind that changes direction with the change of seasons. Monsoons occur mostly in the Indian Ocean, though also in weaker forms in other parts of the world.

Monsoons blow from the southwest, usually from April to October, and from the northeast from October to April. The southwestern monsoon brings the heavy rains that are so important for irrigating land, growing crops, and bringing water to people in India.

Around May or June, the wet season begins. Arriving with violent thunderstorms and refreshingly welcome rain, the monsoon moves up from the south and across the rest of India. It lasts until September or October, bringing the rain that is so essential to growing crops. Areas of heaviest precipitation are the Western Ghats and northeastern parts of India. Cherrapunji, in Assam State, is one of the wettest places on earth. Its annual rainfall is about 450 inches (1,143 cm).

Because its climate can be so extreme, India often suffers from natural disasters, especially droughts and floods. Some droughts have even lasted a few years, ruining crops and causing starvation. Most coastal towns and cities flood during the monsoon, forcing people to slosh through waist-high, brackish water to get from place to place. Sometimes these floods can be very serious, covering roads and railway lines, and even sweeping away people's homes.

When cyclones hit eastern India in September and October, they can cause severe flooding that destroys lives and homes. A devastating cyclone hit eastern India in October 1999. By the time the rubble was cleared away, nearly 10,000 people had died, and about 15 million had lost their homes.

Palm Trees
to Peacocks

INDIA IS ONE OF THE MOST POPULATED COUNTRIES IN THE world, but despite all the people, there is room for plants and animals, too. More than 500 species of mammal roam across the subcontinent, and about 2,000 types of bird nest in the treetops and fly through the skies. Indian waters hold about 2,550 fish species, while any number of reptiles and amphibians make their homes on land and in water. Vegetation ranges from massive trees to the most delicate flowers. Altogether, India can boast of more than 15,000 species of plants.

Rubber trees are common in parts of the south.

Teak, Mangroves, and Eucalyptus

Although much of India used to be covered by trees, people cleared most of them, either for wood or to make space for farming. Now forests cover only about 10 percent of the whole country. Forests are scattered throughout India, from the Deccan Plateau in the south to the jungles in the northeast.

Forests in the south are known for their teak and rosewood trees. These are sturdy trees with very hard wood that is used to make furniture. Wild teak is usually stronger than teak grown on plantations, so many people still cut these trees despite laws that prohibit it.

Banyan Trees

The banyan, or Indian fig tree, is India's national tree. This graceful, shade-giving tree has a special way of supporting itself as it grows. As it spreads, the branches of the banyan dip down and root themselves as new trees over a large area. These roots continue to spread, sprouting more trunks and branches over a long period of time. Looking at an old banyan tree is like looking at a small forest—until you realize that all the branches are connected.

Because they constantly renew themselves, banyan trees are considered immortal and are mentioned in many Indian myths and legends. Banyan trees grow all over India, and village councils often meet in their cool, welcome shade.

Eucalyptus trees and bamboo also grow freely in these forests. Eucalyptus trees have thin, green leaves and soft, peeling bark. They grow well at the higher altitudes of the Eastern and Western Ghat foothills. Bamboo usually grows in clusters called brakes. Because bamboo is so light but strong, people have all kinds of uses for it, from making furniture to building houses.

At lower altitudes, there are thicker, wetter forests. Here, the bamboo is often denser, and long, green vines drape from the trees. Delicate, pinkish orchids blossom on the tree trunks, their heavy roots hanging in the air to absorb water. Sal trees also grow in these tropical forests. They are semi-evergreen trees that can withstand small fires, remaining standing even after everything else has burned down.

Mangrove forests exist only in places that are very wet. These are dense, shady swamps made up of brackish pools and the thick roots of mangrove trees. Mangroves are trees or shrubs that can grow only in shallow, salty water. Their roots form thick, tangled masses that arch above the water. One of the largest mangrove forests is in the Sundarbans National Park in West Bengal. It extends over an area of 1,646 square miles (4,263 sq km).

Along the Coasts

The tropical sea breezes on India's western and eastern coasts provide a warm climate for a large number of plants. The most common tree along the coasts is the coco palm tree. At the top of its long, gnarled trunk, this palm sprouts wide, fringed leaves and clusters of juicy coconuts.

Rubber trees are common on the flatlands in the southern state of Kerala. They grow both in the wild and on plantations. Their leaves look like outstretched, round-fingered hands. People tap the sap from rubber trees and use it to make rubber.

The chembarathy is a flower that grows everywhere along the southern coasts. It has a very bright, red blossom that is easily spotted and very beautiful. It grows in all kinds of places, from wild forests to the backyards of settled towns.

The Lotus

The lotus, or water lily, is the national flower of India. It is a water plant with delicate, pink-white petals. Its blossoms and leaves float on top of shallow water, while its roots disappear below the surface. The many petals of a lotus overlap in intricate patterns, creating a graceful, cupped blossom. Prized for its serenity and grace, the lotus is sacred to both Hindus and Buddhists.

High in the Mountains

High in the Himalaya, many kinds of flowers, shrubs, and trees grow at all times of the year. Alpine meadows burst into bloom with poppies, lilies, larkspurs, and geraniums. Orchids hang from tree trunks, and rhododendrons dot the hillsides. Tea grows wild in certain places in the state of Assam. Although domestic tea shrubs are kept pruned back to 3 to 5 feet (0.9 to 1.5 m), wild shrubs can grow up to 30 feet (9.1 m) high.

Mountain forests sprout mostly evergreen trees, such as pines, fir, and spruce. There are also birch trees, and the deodar, which is a particular kind of cedar tree. Bamboo grows in the mountains, too. Some people in the state of Sikkim make their houses out of bamboo's strong, lightweight stalks.

Birch trees grow in India's mountain forests.

Animals in the Wild

Most wild animals in India are confined to national parks and wildlife sanctuaries, where they can live without the threat of being killed. Thanks to these sanctuaries, a huge and varied number of animals are still found in the nation.

National Parks and Wildlife Sanctuaries

In an effort to preserve India's disappearing wildlife, the Indian government has set aside land where plants and animals can thrive without fear of human disturbance. About 66 national parks and 400 wildlife sanctuaries exist in India today.

The Sasan Gir Lion Sanctuary in the state of Gujarat contains the last remaining population of Asiatic lions in the entire world. The Kaziranga National Park in Assam provides a home for endangered Indian rhinoceroses. Other major national parks include the Sundarbans Wildlife Sanctuary in West Bengal, the Corbett National Park in Uttar Pradesh, and the Periyar Wildlife Sanctuary on the border of Kerala and Tamil Nadu in the south.

Tigers

The Royal Bengal tiger is India's national animal. Bengal tigers live deep in the forests and jungles of India, mostly on nature preserves. Their thick, golden yellow fur is patterned with black stripes that help them blend into the underbrush. Each tiger has its own unique pattern of stripes, like a human fingerprint. Tigers are shy and usually live alone. Their strength and grace have earned them great respect throughout the world.

Bengal tigers were almost completely wiped out due to hunting and habitat destruction. Their numbers shrank from about 100,000 in 1900 to less than 2,000 in 1970. In 1973, an important conservation program called Project Tiger was launched to protect the remaining tigers in India. This project created several nature reserves where tigers could live in peace and safety. Since this project began, the number of tigers in India has risen to about 4,000.

Two of the better-known animals in India are the Royal Bengal tiger and the Indian elephant. Both live in protected forests and jungles, on the southern Deccan Plateau and in the north. Tigers are very shy and are hardly ever seen by humans. Indian elephants, however, are a bit more visible. They are sometimes seen in herds, crossing rivers in late afternoon or grazing in misty meadows at dawn.

Another large rare animal is the Indian rhinoceros, with a population of only about 2,400. This rhino, which has one horn, lives in the far northeastern jungles in the state of Assam. Far to the west lives another very rare animal, the Indian wild ass, with a population of about 2,000. This animal looks like a donkey and lives only in the Little Rann of Kutch, a salt plain along the border between India and Pakistan.

A number of animals graze the Indian wilderness. These include spotted deer, blackbucks, gaurs, and the Nilgiri tahrs in the hills of south India. Gazelles live mostly in the Thar Desert, where they are sometimes spotted bounding gracefully away into the distance.

Despite their shrunken numbers, a few other large animals can still be found in India. Some leopards remain hidden in the forests and mountains. The shy and endangered snow leopard roams the high reaches of the Himalaya, along with the elusive, raccoonlike red panda and the Asiatic black bear. A few Indian gray wolves continue to wander the dry plains of north India, joined by the remaining hyenas and jackals.

There are plenty of monkeys, however. Black langurs and rare golden langurs clamber high in the treetops of both northern and southern forests. Hanuman langurs often cluster around Hindu temples, where they are held sacred because they resemble Hanuman, the Hindu monkey god. Rhesus macaques are the most plentiful monkeys in India. These agile, expressive monkeys can live anywhere, from the rooftops and alleys of towns to boulders and trees in the wild.

Many smaller animals inhabit the Indian wilderness as well. The pale hedgehog, the Bengal fox, the Indian porcupine,

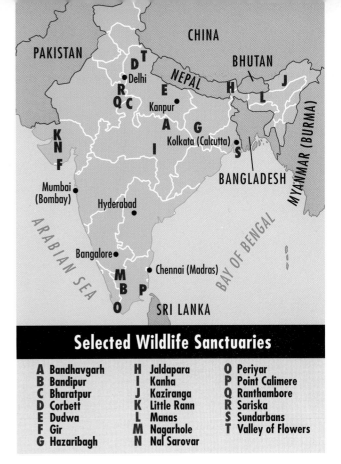

Selected Wildlife Sanctuaries

A	Bandhavgarh	H	Jaldapara	O	Periyar
B	Bandipur	I	Kanha	P	Point Calimere
C	Bharatpur	J	Kaziranga	Q	Ranthambore
D	Corbett	K	Little Rann	R	Sariska
E	Dudwa	L	Manas	S	Sundarbans
F	Gir	M	Nagarhole	T	Valley of Flowers
G	Hazaribagh	N	Nal Sarovar		

A golden langur

Mongooses eat more than just cobras.

and the Indian giant squirrel are only a few. Rats and mice are as common as mongooses. The mongoose is famous for its ability to kill dangerous cobra snakes. Fights between mongooses and cobras are often staged as street shows in India, but in the wild, cobras are really only a small part of the mongoose's diet. They eat mainly rodents, birds, insects, and even fruit.

Some of the birds in India include peacocks, cranes, kingfishers, peregrine falcons, pheasants, cuckoos, and storks. The Bharatpur National Park in Rajasthan is the largest and most spectacular bird sanctuary in the country, with more than 300 species of bird.

Peacocks

India's national bird is the peacock. Peacocks usually live in jungle lands near water or as domestic animals in villages. The female, or peahen, is plain brown, but the male is a fantastic, brilliant blue. He has a huge, fanlike tail patterned with round designs that look somewhat like eyes. Male peacocks spread this magnificent tail whenever they want to attract females, or even just to show off. Peacocks were once bred for food, but now it is illegal to hunt them in India.

Animals Among People

Everywhere you go in India, you see animals. Whether it is chickens pecking in someone's front yard or two bullocks pulling a hay-laden cart down the road, the presence of animals is an essential part of Indian life.

Walking through towns and villages, you will come across goats, pigs, water buffalo, donkeys, dogs, cats, and cows. Cows are sacred to Hindus, many of whom refuse to eat their meat. Although some cows are owned and used for milk production or pulling plows, others are allowed to wander in the streets. Cows are found in many places, even in the large cities of Delhi and Mumbai. They either eat garbage or wait for handouts from generous people.

Other domestic animals in India are camels, yaks, and elephants. Camels are the main transportation in the desert. Yaks are used as pack animals high in the snowy Himalaya, because their long, shaggy hair helps them withstand the extreme cold there. Although it is rare now, elephants are sometimes used as transportation as well. Many centuries ago, people used elephants in the army, either to transport supplies or to carry soldiers into battle.

A cow eating discarded flowers in the city of Varanasi, on the Ganges River

From the
Beginning

HUMAN CIVILIZATION IN INDIA DATES BACK MORE THAN 4,000 years. From the beginning, Indian history has been a record of invasions, wars, and great dynasties that have risen and fallen, making way for the next rulers. Each group that came to India brought its own customs that were woven together to create the complex society that is India today.

Early Civilizations

Traces of the first settled civilizations in India have been found in two areas, both dating back to around 2500 B.C. One civilization formed in south and central India with a group of people called the Dravidians. Descendants of those people still live in southern India today. The other civilization began in the Indus Valley, in what is now Pakistan. That civilization flourished in this valley for about 1,000 years.

In the 1920s, archeologists uncovered the remains of two cities that had been built by the people of the Indus Valley. Known as Harappa and Mohenjo-Daro, these cities show signs of an organized and complex society. Well-built brick houses, paved streets, decorated pottery, and a written language have all been found in these ruins.

Scholars believe that priests ruled this society and that there was an organized system of rules and customs.

The Coming of the Aryans

Between 1500 and 200 B.C., tribes of lighter-skinned people swept down from central Asia and settled in the Indus Valley. These people from central Europe and Asia are known as Aryans, which means "noble ones."

The Aryans spread throughout northern India, moving as far south as the Vindhya hills. Although many were cattle-raising wanderers, some settled in villages. They invaded the civilization in the Indus Valley, and they pushed the Dravidians farther south. The people who stayed became part of the Aryan way of life. In return, the Aryans adopted some of the customs of the people they had conquered. This combination of Aryan society with the society of the original settlers produced the beginnings of Indian culture as it exists today. The Aryans also developed the Sanskrit language, one of the oldest languages in existence.

When the Aryans conquered the people of the Indus Valley, they became the rulers. They set up a caste system with different levels of society.

The Aryans' religious beliefs developed into the basis of the Hindu religion. Aryans combined their gods with those of the people they had conquered. The gods Shiva, Kali, and Brahma have their roots in Aryan civilization. The Aryans also recorded the Vedas, the first sacred Hindu scriptures. The Vedas focus on religious rituals, ideas of social order, and the origins of the universe.

More Invasions

King Porus surrendering to
Alexander the Great

Other invaders of ancient India included the Persians and the
Greeks. In 518 B.C., King Darius of Persia marched into India.
He conquered both the Indus Valley and West Punjab, which
his armies ruled until his death.

In 327 B.C., Alexander the Great of Macedonia overthrew
King Darius's descendant, Darius III, then defeated a king
named Porus and marched as far as the Beas River. However,
the Indians fought back so fiercely that Alexander the Great
was forced to turn back and leave India altogether.

The reports of India's fertility and riches that Alexander's
army brought back helped spark European interest in India.
Kings and explorers began to think about opportunities for trade.

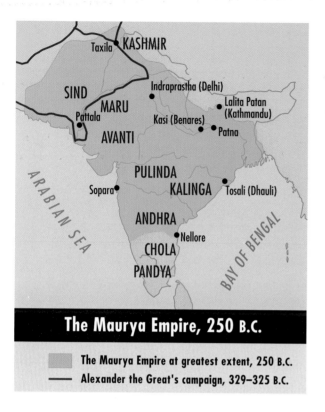

The Maurya Empire, 250 B.C.

- The Maurya Empire at greatest extent, 250 B.C.
— Alexander the Great's campaign, 329–325 B.C.

The Maurya Empire

Two hundred years before Alexander invaded, an Indian kingdom had started to develop in the north. After Alexander left, this kingdom expanded. The first major ruler of this first great Indian empire was called Chandragupta. The empire came to be known as the Maurya Empire.

The Mauryas ruled for about 140 years. Building their capital at present-day Patna, they eventually spread across most of northern India. They had a huge army, an organized government, and a strict system of tax collection. Although the nobles led comfortable lives, everyday life for the peasants remained harsh.

The Maurya Empire reached its peak under Emperor Ashoka, the last great ruler of the dynasty. It began to fall apart after his death in 232 B.C. By 184 B.C., the empire had collapsed completely.

Emperor Ashoka

Ashoka was born about 291 B.C. He became emperor of the Mauryas in 269 B.C. He fought wars, conquered other groups, and expanded his empire. However, in 262 B.C., after witnessing the brutality of war, Ashoka converted to Buddhism and stopped the violence in his leadership. His new administration focused on love and tolerance for their fellow men, even for those Ashoka had conquered. He built Buddhist shrines all over India and sent Buddhist missionaries to such countries as Sri Lanka and Burma. Ashoka built cave temples for Buddhist monks as well as *stupas*—semicircular mounds of brick where relics of the Buddha were kept. One of his symbols, the Lion of Sarnath, is now the national symbol of independent India.

The Rise of the Guptas

After the Mauryas, northern India split into hundreds of separate kingdoms. Foreign invaders ruled over much of northern and central India. This lasted until A.D. 319, when a king named Chandragupta I founded the Gupta Empire by reuniting a large part of India. The Guptas eventually spread across northern India as far west as the Arabian Sea.

The Gupta Empire reached its peak during the reign of Chandragupta's grandson, Chandragupta II, who is also called Samudragupta. Chandragupta II reigned from 330 to about 375. He built universities and encouraged art and science among his subjects. Painting, literature, and sculpture flourished, as did science. During Chandragupta II's reign, scientific accomplishments include the mathematical term *zero* and the discovery that the world was round.

The Gupta Empire lasted until around 550, when it was defeated by the White Huns from central Asia. After the empire's defeat, it was gradually broken up into many separate Hindu kingdoms.

The South

During these years, changes were also occurring in southern India. South of the Vindhya Range, dynasties were rising and falling independently from those in the north. The major southern empires included the Cholas, the Pandyas, the Cheras, the Chalukyas, and the Pallavas.

A bronze sculpture of the Buddha from the Gupta Empire

Saint Thomas appearing on the shore of India

Hinduism was the main religion in the south, although many villagers still worshiped nature gods. Christianity came to southern India in A.D. 52, when Saint Thomas the Apostle landed in modern-day Kerala. Although many people remained Hindus, a large part of the local population converted to Christianity. Kerala is still known for its strong Christian influence.

Islam and India

Although a few Muslim invaders had already conquered parts of India, Islam made its first strong impact around 977, with the bandit raids of Sabuktigin of Ghazni. In 1192, Muslims marched into India again. The new ruler of Ghazni, Mohammed of Ghori, moved first into the Punjab, where he defeated the Indian king, Prithviraj Chauhan, at Tarain. He founded a kingdom that gradually spread across the Ganges plain and lasted for more than 300 years. The Muslim sultans who ruled this kingdom built their capital at present-day Delhi, which would remain the capital of many empires to come.

Although the Muslims destroyed many Hindu temples and statues when they invaded, they were more tolerant during their actual rule. Both Hindus and Muslims continued to practice their own customs, with little interference on either side.

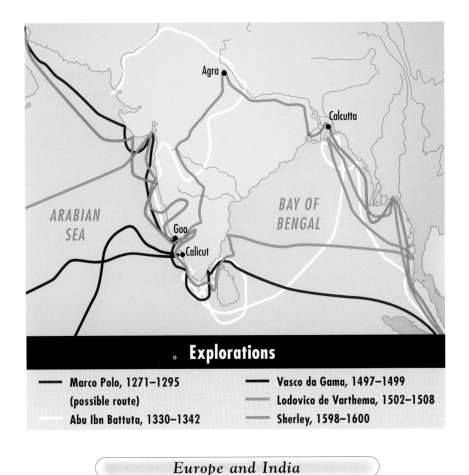

Explorations

- —— Marco Polo, 1271–1295 (possible route)
- —— Abu Ibn Battuta, 1330–1342
- —— Vasco da Gama, 1497–1499
- —— Lodovico de Varthema, 1502–1508
- —— Sherley, 1598–1600

Europe and India

One of the first European explorers to set foot in India was the Italian traveler Marco Polo. His initial voyage was to China in the thirteenth century, where he soon became a favorite of Kublai Khan. The khan sent Polo on many expeditions around Asia, including to India. When Polo traveled to India, he was impressed by its wealthy and advanced civilization. His reports were the first real information about India to reach Europe.

Europeans began to hunger for the rich silks and exotic spices that Polo had described. Other explorers set out to discover a sea route directly to India. A Portuguese sailor named

Vasco da Gama with an Indian ruler, the Zamorin of Calicut

Vasco da Gama sailed around the Cape of Good Hope at the tip of Africa and then across the Indian Ocean. In 1498, he landed on the shores of present-day Kerala. His expedition opened the way for future European explorers.

The South Again

Around this time, dynasties in the south were shifting once more. Among the fragmented mass of kingdoms, a new empire began to form. This was the Hindu empire of Vijayanagar, founded in 1336 at the site of modern-day Hampi in the state of Karnataka. The Vijayanagar Empire was the strongest Hindu kingdom at the time, when most of the north was under the rule of Muslim sultans. This empire lasted until 1565, when its army was defeated in the Battle of Talikota by Muslims from Bijapur.

The Mughals

In 1526, India came under a new Muslim influence from central Asia. Mongols invaded northern India and founded the Mughal Empire. The leader was called Babur. He was the first in a long line of successful emperors. Over a period of about 200 years, the Mughal Empire spread over all of northern India, parts of southern India, Afghanistan, and present-day Pakistan and Bangladesh. It had capitals in Agra and Delhi.

Despite their power, the Mughals did not destroy the existing ways of life in the lands they conquered. In return for their protection, they demanded a payment of taxes and soldiers for their armies. They left local governments in the control of the people who lived there.

The Mughals had a passion for building. They erected immense and beautiful buildings, many of which still stand. The Red Fort in Delhi was constructed during this time, as was the famous Taj Mahal, built by Emperor Shah Jahan as a tomb for his favorite wife.

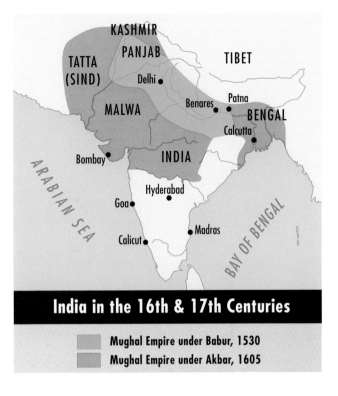

India in the 16th & 17th Centuries

Mughal Empire under Babur, 1530

Mughal Empire under Akbar, 1605

Delhi's Red Fort was built by the Mughals.

Akbar crossing the Ganges

There were many great Mughal emperors. Akbar was considered the greatest ruler. Reigning from 1556 to 1605, he combined military ability with religious tolerance and a taste for culture. At his court, Akbar encouraged lively discussions among members of all religions, from Hindus and Muslims to Christians. Akbar also ended the tax on Hindus that previous rulers had demanded. The other Mughal rulers were Humayun, Jehangir, Shah Jahan, and Aurangzeb.

Revolts, from both outside and within the kingdom, eventually weakened the empire. Although Mughal rulers continued to reign over kingdoms throughout India, the empire had crumbled by the 1800s.

Conflicting Powers

When Vasco da Gama returned to Europe laden with spices, cotton, silks, and indigo from India, other Europeans began to dream about the wealth awaiting them in that distant land. Portugal was one of the first countries to establish trading posts along India's western coast. In 1510, the Portuguese captured the present-day state of Goa, which they would control until 1961. Denmark and Holland followed Portugal's example, setting up small trading posts of their own. France established a large trading post at Pondicherry in 1672.

In 1600, Queen Elizabeth I of England allowed a private company, the East India Company, to set up trade in India. It was this company that would govern British actions in India for the next 250 years. In 1611, the East India Company set up its first trading post at Machlipatanam, and then a second one in 1612 at Surat. More trading posts were established later.

For the most part, local Indian rulers did not oppose these trading posts. Trade with Europe brought them valuable gold and silver to enrich their treasuries. Besides, there was no central Indian government to resist the Europeans.

The British built their Madras trading post in 1640.

Robert Clive

Born in England on September 29, 1725, Robert Clive joined the East India Company when he was only eighteen. Although he began as a clerk, Clive rose quickly to the military rank of captain. He led battles against the French and their Indian allies in order to secure British power in India. Clive's most famous battle was the Battle of Plassey in 1757. He led a British and Indian army of less than 3,000 soldiers against Siraj-ud-daula, the Nawab of Bengal, and his army of 50,000 soldiers. Clive's victory over Siraj-ud-daula paved the way for further British expansion into India.

Clive returned briefly to England, where he joined Parliament and was knighted. He returned to India in 1765 as governor and commander in chief of Bengal. Clive worked for the East India Company until his death in 1774.

Great Britain and France struggled to gain a solid foothold in India. They pitted local rulers against each other. If the British opposed one Indian ruler, the French would supply that ruler with weapons in an effort to defeat the British.

After the 1763 peace treaty to end the Seven Years' War, the French kept only a few trading centers in India. However, the British continued to fight the French in India. In 1799, the British finally crushed most of France's power in India by killing the French-supported ruler of Mysore, Tipu Sultan. After this victory, the British defeated the Marathas in 1803 and the Sikhs in the Punjab in 1849, and made peace with the Gurkhas in Nepal in 1818. Slowly but surely, Britain was well on its way to securing an Indian empire.

British India

By the early nineteenth century, Great Britain controlled almost the entire subcontinent under the administration of the East India Company. The company was ruled by governors-general appointed by the British government. The East

India Company controlled about half of India, while the other half was left in the hands of Indian princes who had pledged loyalty to Great Britain.

The British caused many changes in India. Some of these changes were helpful to Indians, and some were not. They built schools and hospitals, paved roads, and laid down the framework for the huge Indian railway system. They created the Indian Civil Service, which gave Indians secure, well-paying jobs. However, the British government also passed the Permanent Settlement Act of 1793. This law stated that if a landowner was unable to pay taxes on his land, then that land would be taken away. Although the purpose of this act was to ensure payment of taxes to the British, it created a large class of landless peasants. Lord Cornwallis, the governor-general from 1786 to 1793, passed a law that kept Indians from high posts in the government. This led to a huge gap between the British and their Indian subjects. British settlements were prosperous towns, but many Indians were forced to live in slums. On top of this, many of the British rulers were insensitive to Indian practices and traditions that were different from English customs.

By the mid-nineteenth century, the East India Company controlled even more of India. While India had been relatively wealthy and advanced in the 1600s, this had changed by the 1800s. After the breakup of the Mughal Empire and the southern kingdoms, most of Indian civilization fell into ruin. Much of the wealth was either pocketed by the remaining Indian nobles or taken out of India by corrupt British merchants of the East India Company.

The Industrial Revolution in England also led to Indian discontentment under British rule. Cloth made cheaply and quickly in England was sent to India. More expensive Indian goods were neglected, and many Indian craftspeople went out of business. All of this caused unhappiness and unrest among many Indians.

In 1857, the Indians rebelled. A rumor spread among Indian soldiers, or *sepoys*, in the British armies that their bullets had been greased with animal fat. Some said it was pig fat, while others thought it was from cows. Pigs are unclean to Muslims, and cows are holy to Hindus, so everybody considered this an insult. This rumor, combined with general discontent with British rule, led to the Sepoy Mutiny of 1857.

Soldiers rebelled all across northern India, fighting battles in which many Indians and British were killed.

When the uprising was finally crushed in 1858, the British made a decision. The East India Company was taken apart, and power was handed over to the British government. India was now one of the brightest jewels in the British crown.

British forces storming Delhi during the Sepoy Mutiny

Toward Independence

For a generation after the Sepoy Mutiny of 1857, British rule in India was at its peak. Queen Victoria was named Empress of India in 1877, while her British subjects gloried in their rule over the people of India. But by the end of the nineteenth century, this began to change.

Among Indians, a new sense of nationalism was developing. The country became more unified in opposition to British rule. They began to desire their own nation, without British control.

In 1885, the India National Congress was formed. At first, this organization was a small political club of educated, middle-class Indians who met to discuss possible reforms. Over time, it turned into a political party that openly opposed British rule.

In 1906, a number of Muslims split from the Hindu-dominated congress and formed the All-India Muslim League. This group fought for the rights of Muslims, and eventually it began to fight for its own Muslim nation as well. The British now had two strong forces against them.

A few British leaders began to discuss giving control to Indians, and in 1917, the British Parliament issued a declaration for eventual self-rule in India. However, the government also passed laws that suspended Indians' civil rights and restricted political activities in India, which increased anger against the British.

Around this time, a new leader emerged. He was Mohandas Karamchand Gandhi, a lawyer from a wealthy

Hindu family in Gujarat. In 1915, he returned to India after spending many years fighting for Indian rights in South Africa. He dedicated his life to fighting for India's independence. Gandhi used a nonviolent method of passive resistance, called *satyagraha* in Hindi. His resistance included peaceful marches, hunger strikes, and refusing to buy British goods. Gandhi began the *swadeshi* movement, which encouraged Indians to spin their own cloth rather than buy machine-made British cloth. His peaceful nature and strength of will earned Gandhi the name *Mahatma*, which means "Great Soul."

Frustrated by this opposition to their rule, the British became stricter. In 1919, the British army fired on a peaceful Indian protest in the city of Amritsar. About 400 Indians were killed, and about 1,200 were wounded. The Amritsar Massacre turned people all around the world against the British control of India.

The Independence Movement gathered force and speed. Leaders were often jailed for their peaceful resistance. Gandhi himself spent several years in prison. Many others joined him, including Motilal Nehru and his son, Jawaharlal Nehru, two leaders important in the fight for independence. In 1929, Jawaharlal Nehru was elected president of the India National Congress.

The British slowly began to give in. In 1935, the British government passed the Government of India Act, which laid down the framework for self-government. The law went into effect in 1937, giving hope to India's desire for independence. The long road to freedom seemed to be nearing its end.

The Salt March of 1930

Mahatma Gandhi's peaceful methods of protest gained world-wide fame in 1930. Frustrated by the heavy taxes that the British put on salt, Gandhi led a march to the seashore to make salt rather than being forced to buy it at such high prices. He began with seventy-eight followers, but by the end of the 240-mile (386-km) march, thousands of people had joined him. By making their own salt, these Indians broke British law. Gandhi was arrested and spent eight months in prison. This action only brought more attention to the Independence Movement, however, and gained Gandhi and his followers more public support.

Independence

When World War II ended in 1945, Great Britain was exhausted. With its economy shaken, it no longer had the strength to hold its empire together. Britain declared that India would become an independent dominion within the British Commonwealth.

On August 15, 1947, India celebrated its first Independence Day with huge parties and booming fireworks. However, it was not to be a completely joyful occasion.

For many years before 1947, Muslims had been pushing for their own nation, separate from Hindu-dominated India. When independence was granted, the British also granted Muslims their wish. India was cut apart in an act that came to be known as Partition, and West Pakistan and East Pakistan were created as new homes for India's huge Muslim population.

Independence in 1947

La DOMENICA DEL CORRIERE

Deadly fighting between Hindus and Muslims followed Partition.

After Partition, the fighting between Hindus and Muslims rose to tragic levels. Riots broke out as Muslims in India tried to flee to Pakistan. Hindus caught in Pakistan surged toward the Indian border. Many violent acts were committed on both sides during the next few years. When the riots were finally over, nearly a million people had been killed.

Saddened by the warfare, Gandhi traveled from one area to another to discuss his peaceful ideas. Some Hindus began to think Gandhi was too sympathetic toward the Muslims. On January 30, 1948, the Mahatma was shot to death by a Hindu fanatic. Gandhi lived to see his beloved India become independent, but he was killed less than six months later.

Dr. B. R. Ambedkar

B. R. Ambedkar was born in 1891 in modern-day Maharashtra. He became a lawyer and soon entered politics. Dr. Ambedkar was independent India's first law minister, and he helped write the constitution in 1950. Born an "untouchable," or outcaste, in Hindu society, Dr. Ambedkar devoted his life to helping other untouchables. He helped pass many laws that made it easier for untouchables (now called *Dalits*, or scheduled castes) to receive education and jobs. In 1956, he converted to Buddhism to protest the Hindu caste system. Nearly a million untouchables followed his lead. He died in 1956 and is still referred to lovingly as *Babasaheb* or Baba Ambedkar.

A New Democracy

Although India had won its independence, its people were not satisfied with the position of their country as a dominion of Great Britain. They wanted to be more independent. On January 26, 1950, a new constitution was adopted, making India the first republic in the British Commonwealth.

Jawaharlal Nehru had already been appointed prime minister of India. He now set out to solve the problems of his new nation. Nehru began a series of five-year plans targeted at industrializing India. By introducing modern methods of technology, Nehru hoped to raise the standard of living for all Indians.

Nehru practiced a policy of keeping India neutral in world affairs. However, the nation continued to have problems with its neighbors. In 1962, India fought a war with China when Chinese armies crossed the border in the northeast and into Ladakh. In 1965, another clash occurred between India and Pakistan, over Kashmir in the northwest. Although Kashmir was given to India during Partition, many Pakistanis believed it should be a part of Pakistan because of its high Muslim population. The dispute continues to this day.

When Nehru died in 1964, Lal Bahadur Shastri briefly took over the position of prime minister. In 1966, Nehru's daughter, Indira Gandhi (no relation to the Mahatma) became India's third prime minister. Indira Gandhi promoted agricultural reforms to improve rural areas. In 1971, she led India to victory in another war with Pakistan. This war granted East Pakistan independence from West Pakistan, and it was renamed Bangladesh. India was recognized as the most powerful nation in southern Asia.

Indira Gandhi became prime minister in 1966.

In 1974, however, Indira Gandhi's popularity shrank when the prices of goods shot up. In protest, workers went on strike, and students began to demand higher wages for workers. In 1974, the government tested nuclear devices, which only increased public protest against the government that could afford to test missiles but not to pay its workers higher wages. In 1975, Indira Gandhi declared a state of emergency to silence her political opposition. Civil rights were suspended, and many of her enemies were jailed. Even though she used this period of time to bring prices down and increase the production of crops and manufactured goods, many Indians still disagreed with her methods. When elections were held again in 1977, the people voted against her.

In 1984, Indira Gandhi sent army troops to the Golden Temple in Amritsar.

Indira Gandhi rallied her forces and came back to power in 1980. In 1984, she sent the Indian army to suppress members of the Sikh religion that were holding out in the Sikh's holiest shrine, the Golden Temple in Amritsar. These Sikhs wanted the government to provide them with their own state in the northwest of India. That move was to be her undoing. In October 1984, Gandhi was killed by her own bodyguards, two Sikhs angry at the desecration of their religion's holiest place.

Her son Rajiv Gandhi was voted to fill her place as prime minister. He introduced more technology into India, which helped the middle class in the cities and brought India into more contact with the rest of the world. However, he lost power in 1989 because of corruption scandals. He was assassinated in 1991 by terrorists at an election rally.

Since the end of the Nehru-Gandhi line, other politicians have gained power in the Indian government. Each leader has had to deal with such recurring problems as poverty, overpopulation, and continuing hatred among Hindus, Muslims, and Sikhs. India continues to battle with Pakistan over the control of Kashmir. In December 1992, in the small town of Ayodhya in Uttar Pradesh, devout Hindus destroyed a Muslim mosque that Hindus believed was built on the site of an ancient Hindu temple. Riots broke out between Muslims and Hindus that killed several hundred people.

Rajiv Gandhi campaigning

Despite these problems, however, India has grown rapidly since it won its independence. Crop production has increased, roads have been improved, new railway lines built, and an extensive telephone system installed. India launched its first communication satellite, *Aryabhata*, in 1972. In 1984, Rakesh Sharma became the first Indian in space when he flew on board the Russian Soyuz T-11 spacecraft. India is also one of the few countries to have developed a nuclear bomb. Further testing of nuclear missiles was carried out in 1998. Medical achievements have also increased. Researchers are even developing a vaccine against leprosy, a serious disease that destroys nerve endings in humans.

The World's Largest Democracy

A voter casts her ballot.

E VER SINCE INDIA ADOPTED ITS CONSTITUTION ON January 26, 1950, it has been the most populated democracy in the world. Indians enjoy widespread voting rights and freedom of speech, religion, and the press. India is formally called a Sovereign Socialist Secular Democratic Republic. It has a parliamentary system of government with three main branches—executive, legislative, and judicial. Compared with other democracies such as the United States, India has a central government that exercises more power in relation to its states. The nation also has two main leaders—a prime minister and a president.

Opposite: **The Secretariat, a government building in New Delhi**

The World's Largest Democracy **57**

The National Flag

India's flag was designed when the nation won its independence from Great Britain. Its three horizontal bars are saffron, white, and green. The color saffron stands for courage and sacrifice. The white band in the middle represents purity and truth, and green symbolizes faith and fertility. The flag has a blue wheel in the center called the Dharma Chakra that was designed by Emperor Ashoka many centuries ago. It stands for the importance of law and duty in all life. This wheel also recalls the spinning wheel that Mahatma Gandhi encouraged Indians to use to make cloth so that they would not have to depend on British goods anymore.

Executive Branch

The Indian government administers its power in the name of its president. The president and the vice president are both elected indirectly by a special electoral college. They serve five-year terms, but the vice president does not automatically become president if the president dies or is removed from office.

Jawaharlal Nehru

Jawaharlal Nehru was born in 1889. He became a lawyer after graduating from Harrow and Cambridge in England. Nehru turned to nationalism in 1919, after the British massacre of peaceful protesters in Amritsar. He worked closely with Mahatma Gandhi to make India independent and was elected president of the India National Congress in 1929. After independence, Nehru became India's first prime minister. He encouraged the use of technology in the new nation, causing many factories and roads to be built. Nehru served as prime minister until his death in 1964.

However, the president's role in the government is mostly ceremonial. The real power is in the hands of the prime minister, who heads the Council of Ministers, or cabinet. Members of Parliament elect the prime minister after the legislative elections. In the years since independence, India's prime ministers have made the real decisions for the nation.

Legislative Branch

The Indian legislature is patterned after Great Britain's parliamentary system. India's Parliament is split into two parts, the *Rajya Sabha* (Council of States) and the *Lok Sabha* (Council of the People). The Rajya Sabha has about 250 members, and

A meeting of India's Parliament

the Lok Sabha has 545. The state governments elect most Rajya Sabha members, while the president appoints the remaining members. Except for two members appointed by the president, all the Lok Sabha members are elected directly by the people. The Council of Ministers answers to the Lok Sabha, and therefore to the people.

The Parliament is in charge of the matters that most widely affect the country. It makes decisions concerning such issues as overseas policy, national defense, and national banking.

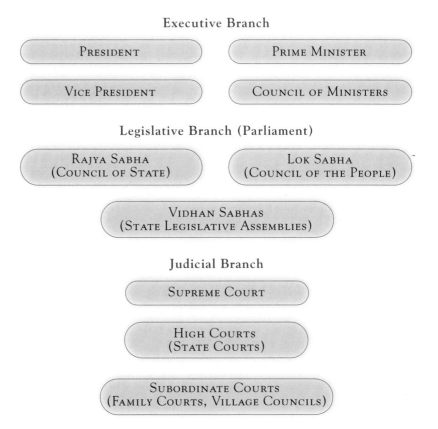

NATIONAL GOVERNMENT OF INDIA

Executive Branch

| President | Prime Minister |
| Vice President | Council of Ministers |

Legislative Branch (Parliament)

| Rajya Sabha (Council of State) | Lok Sabha (Council of the People) |

Vidhan Sabhas (State Legislative Assemblies)

Judicial Branch

Supreme Court

High Courts (State Courts)

Subordinate Courts (Family Courts, Village Councils)

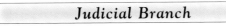

Judicial Branch

Although it is now within the control of independent India, the system of courts and judges began under the British. Its procedures and concepts therefore resemble the judicial systems in many western countries, including Great Britain and the United States.

India's Supreme Court is headed by one chief justice and twenty-five other justices. Every Supreme Court justice is appointed by the president on the advice of the prime minister. It is the job of the Supreme Court and the numerous state courts to translate and enforce the laws of the republic.

State and Local Government

India is made up of twenty-five states and seven union territories. Union territories are islands and large cities that are part of the union without being separate states. Examples of union territories are Chandigarh, Pondicherry, and the Andaman and Nicobar Islands. Although the central government holds more power, state governments are in charge of such matters as local police forces and schools.

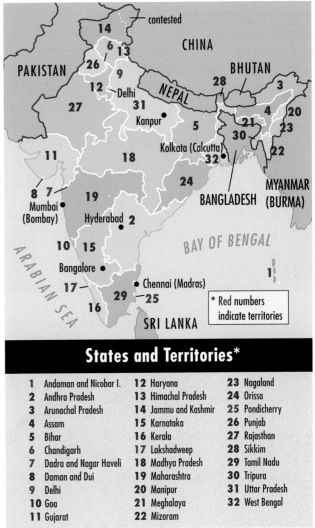

States and Territories*

1	Andaman and Nicobar I.	12	Haryana
2	Andhra Pradesh	13	Himachal Pradesh
3	Arunachal Pradesh	14	Jammu and Kashmir
4	Assam	15	Karnataka
5	Bihar	16	Kerala
6	Chandigarh	17	Lakshadweep
7	Dadra and Nagar Haveli	18	Madhya Pradesh
8	Daman and Diu	19	Maharashtra
9	Delhi	20	Manipur
10	Goa	21	Meghalaya
11	Gujarat	22	Mizoram

23	Nagaland
24	Orissa
25	Pondicherry
26	Punjab
27	Rajasthan
28	Sikkim
29	Tamil Nadu
30	Tripura
31	Uttar Pradesh
32	West Bengal

An outdoor meeting of a panchayat

On a local level, problems are solved by traditional village councils called *panchayats*. They resolve matters such as municipal decisions and arguments over property.

Political Parties

Since the independence movement, the Congress Party has been the most influential political party in India. Some of the nation's strongest prime ministers, including Jawaharlal Nehru and Indira Gandhi, have been members of this party.

In recent years, however, the popularity of the Congress Party has declined. The ruling political party in India today is the Bharatiya Janata Party (BJP).

During the political turmoil of the 1980s and 1990s, many new political parties sprang up. These include the Janata Party, the Janata Dal, and the United Front. None of these lasted very long, however, and the Congress Party and BJP are still the strongest parties. In parts of Kerala and West Bengal, the Communist Party is also popular.

People gathered for an election rally

Although India tries to practice neutrality in world affairs, it must still maintain a large military to protect itself. In fact, India's armed forces are the third largest in the world.

The Indian army employs more than 1 million people. About a quarter of its thirty-four divisions are kept busy along the borders in Kashmir and the northeast, where terrorist activity is common.

India's air force is the world's fourth largest. It is highly equipped, with more than 600 combat aircraft and more than 500 transport aircraft and helicopters.

The Indian navy is much smaller. Both the navy and the small coast guard work hard to patrol the long stretches of India's coastline.

India maintains a large military force.

New Delhi: Did You Know This?

Situated about 656 feet (198 m) above sea level, New Delhi spreads out from the west bank of the Yamuna River, just south of ancient Shahjahanabad (popularly known as Old Delhi). It supports a population of about 350,000. Temperatures in New Delhi range from about 50°F (10°C) in January to around 95°F (35°C) in July.

New Delhi's broad avenues and majestic buildings were designed in 1911. In 1931, the British moved their headquarters from Calcutta and officially named New Delhi their new capital. When India became independent in 1947, ownership of New Delhi passed to the new Indian government.

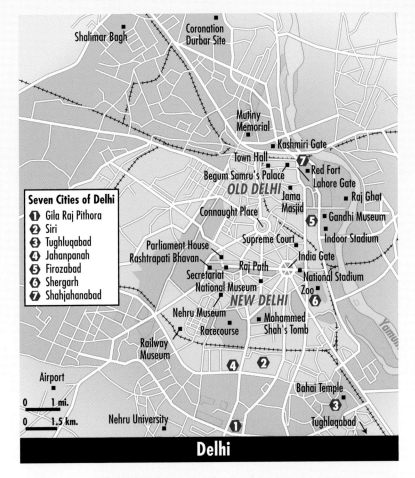

Seven Cities of Delhi
1. Gila Raj Pithora
2. Siri
3. Tughluqabad
4. Jahanpanah
5. Firozabad
6. Shergarh
7. Shahjahanabad

The business district of Connaught Place lies at the north end of New Delhi. It is distinguished by tall, white-columned buildings and a series of circular streets that curve around a busy traffic circle and a large, grassy park. Farther south is the cluster of government buildings, built along the wide avenue called *Raj Path* (King's Way). India Gate, a huge war memorial for Indian soldiers killed in battle, towers at one end of Raj Path. Rashtrapati Bhavan sprawls at the other end. This carefully designed building is the residence of India's president. The Secretariat and Parliament buildings also stand along Raj Path.

The World's Largest Democracy **65**

Earning a Living

OR CENTURIES, INDIA HAS BEEN FAMOUS FOR THE QUALITY
and the variety of the goods it produces. From silks and spices to
rice and cotton, people in India make some of the most prized
products in the world. Through the energetic efforts of such
leaders as Jawaharlal Nehru, India's growing industries have produced a vast array of manufactured goods. India now exports
everything from hand-carved statues and tea to chemicals and
electrical appliances.

Opposite: **Delivering goods
by tricycle cart**

Rich and Poor

As with everything else, India is a land of contrasts when it
comes to wealth. While some Indians are very wealthy, many
are extremely poor. In between
these two extremes is the growing middle class, mostly
businesspeople and their families who have prospered in
India's expanding economy.
Middle-class families enjoy
secure jobs, comfortable homes,
and plenty to eat.

India is a rich country in
many ways. Its vast stretches of
fertile plains provide plenty of
opportunity for farming. Cities

**Shanty homes present a
sharp contrast to high-rises
in Mumbai.**

such as Mumbai and Kolkata have numerous factories and other industries. India is also famous for the rich fabrics and beautiful silver and gold jewelry its people make.

Some Indians become wealthy by exporting Indian products to other countries. Some have important jobs as government officials, and others are rich landlords owning many acres of fertile land. In 1991, new laws allowed foreign companies to build factories and invest in India. The resulting influx of companies, especially computer companies, has provided many jobs for the growing middle class.

Despite all of this, many Indians are still poor. An estimated 35 percent of the population lives below the national poverty line. In poor families, every member of the household who can find a job usually works, sometimes even the children. People in rural areas often suffer from oppressive landlords or natural disasters such as droughts and floods. If their crops fail too often, many of these Indians move to the cities in search of work. Jobs are often hard to find, however, and some people end up sleeping on the street.

Dawn wakes people living on Delhi's streets and rooftops.

To add to these problems, the Indian government is in debt to many countries. Over the years, India has borrowed money from other nations when its own funds were not enough to provide such things as famine relief during a drought. Although India has repaid some of these debts, it is difficult to pay them all when many of its citizens are hungry.

Money Facts

India's basic unit of currency is the rupee. One rupee can be broken down into 100 paise, as a dollar is split into 100 cents. Rupees are issued in 1-, 2-, and 5-rupee coins and in 5-, 10-, 20-, 50-, 100-, and 500-rupee paper notes.

Most rupee notes are printed with a symbol of the Lion of Sarnath. This symbol was designed in the third century B.C. by Emperor Ashoka to represent the peace and goodwill of the Buddha. It shows three lions (with a fourth hidden from view) on a pedestal. Each lion stands for power, confidence, and courage. The animals at the pedestal's base are the guardians of the four directions. They are the lion of the north, the horse of the south, the elephant of the east, and the bull of the west. The motto *Satyameva Jayate* is written in Hindi below the pedestal. It means "Truth alone triumphs."

Most Indian farmers use cattle and water buffalo to pull their plows.

India is often said to be a land of farmers, with about 65 percent of its citizens working as agricultural laborers. Most Indian farmers work very hard. Their farms are usually no larger than 2 acres (0.8 hectares) and often are smaller than 1 acre (0.4 ha). They must use that tiny patch of ground to grow enough food both to feed their families and to have some left over to sell.

Despite these problems, Indian farmers still manage to produce a huge variety of crops. Rice is one of the most important crops. Rice is planted in flooded paddy fields because this crop needs a lot of water in order to grow. Wheat, lentils, cotton, and sugarcane are also grown all over India. Jute is harvested

Women carrying sheaves of wheat

and used to make rope and sacks. Tea is grown on vast plantations in the hills and is one of the nation's largest exports. About 1.5 billion pounds (more than 680 million kilograms) of tea are picked in India each year, and about 800,000 pounds (362,874 kg) of that is exported to other countries.

Some other crops are coffee, tobacco, beans, and spices such as pepper and cardamom. Rubber is manufactured from the rubber trees in the south, and lumber from teak trees is used to make furniture. Other trees are cut down for lumber that is either burned as fuel or used to make houses and other wooden items.

A tea taster at work

Fruits grown in India include pineapples, mangoes, coconuts, watermelons, oranges, bananas, papayas, grapes, and apples. Sometimes people grow these fruits on farms or plantations, but many fruit trees and vines also grow in the wild.

Domestic animals are part of farming in India. Cattle and water buffalo are often used to pull plows or carts laden with harvested crops. Although many Indians do not eat meat, livestock is still important to those who do. The meat that is not eaten is exported to other countries. Indians raise chickens, pigs, goats, sheep, and water buffalo for food. Some people even raise cows for their meat, but most Indians rely on cows only for their milk.

To many of India's leaders, industry has been the key to creating a strong, self-reliant nation. After independence, many new factories were built and modern technology was introduced. India is now a major producer and exporter of manufactured goods.

The textile industry ranks at the top, churning out fabrics and ready-made clothes that are sold all over the world. Leather goods are also a major export, including shoes, handbags, and traditional sandals called *chappals*. Since the 1980s, the production of electronics has also increased. Television sets, computers, and radios are all made in India. India's car industry manufactures a variety of cars, including the Maruti Suzuki, the Ford Ikon, the Tata Indica, the Fiat 110, and the Hindustan Ambassador.

Electronics production contributes to India's economy.

Factories are not the only manufacturers, however. About half of all products made in India are produced by village industries. These small, family-run businesses make everything from shoes and hand-dyed fabrics to carved statues, using skills that have been passed down through each generation. More than 10 million Indians work in these village-based industries.

Although India produces many of its own chemicals and petrochemicals, it must import fertilizers and petroleum products. Other imports include iron, steel, machinery, and precious stones.

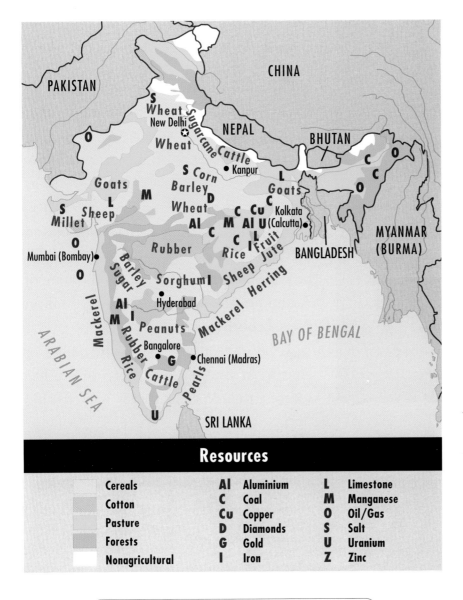

Resources

Cereals	
Cotton	
Pasture	
Forests	
Nonagricultural	

Al	Aluminium	L	Limestone
C	Coal	M	Manganese
Cu	Copper	O	Oil/Gas
D	Diamonds	S	Salt
G	Gold	U	Uranium
I	Iron	Z	Zinc

Mining and Energy

There are about 4,400 mines in India. From these mines come natural resources such as metals and minerals. Coal is the center of the mining industry, and it provides about 60 percent of the nation's energy requirements. Iron ore is also an important resource. Some iron ore is used in India for the production of

An offshore oil rig near Mumbai

steel, while the remainder is exported to other countries. Additional mining products include lead, copper, bauxite, gold, diamonds, zinc, manganese, and limestone.

Although India imports most of its petroleum from the Middle East, it also has oil fields, with an average of 5 billion barrels of oil reserves. The offshore fields near Mumbai and the fields in the state of Assam are the largest producers of oil on the subcontinent.

Coal and oil are the main sources of energy in India, but there are other sources, too. Nuclear power is increasing

What India Grows, Makes, and Mines

Agriculture (1998 est.)

Sugarcane	265,000,000 metric tons
Rice	122,244,000 metric tons
Wheat	66,000,000 metric tons

Manufacturing (1997 est.)

Cement	80,000,000 metic tons
Milled rice	74,485,000 metric tons
Flour	49,500,000 metric tons

Mining (1997 est.)

Iron ore	70,000,000,000 metric tons
Lead	32,000,000,000 metric tons
Zinc	142,000,000 metric tons

as a source of energy. There are now about five nuclear power plants scattered around the country, and the construction of more is planned. The government is also encouraging wind, hydro, and solar power as alternate sources of energy.

Tourism

Over the past few decades, the tourist industry has grown considerably. A 1997 consensus estimated about 2.4 million tourists arrived in India that year, a 35 percent increase from 1993. Altogether, tourists spent around U.S.$3.2 billion within India in 1997.

Tourists travel to India either independently or as part of package tours. Although many people journey all over the country, there are a few main tourist attractions, including the Red Fort in Delhi and the Taj Mahal in Agra.

Tourists visiting a bird sanctuary

How people travel also contributes money to the economy. The transportation system employs many people, from rickshaw drivers to train operators. India has an intricate network of roads and railroads. At least 1,248,742 miles (2,009,660 km) of roads exist throughout India, although half of them are unpaved. Railroads add up to around 38,813 miles (62,464 km) of tracks laid down all across the subcontinent.

Trains are a major mode of transportation. India has a huge and complicated railway system that was started by the British. Most trains run from state to state, but in large cities local trains also go to nearby suburbs. Each train has cars according to different classes, from the standing-room-only, unreserved third class to the comfortably air-conditioned first class. Because most trains take several days to travel long distances, trains have special cars with berths for sleeping.

A busy city train station

Buses provide another way to travel. Although each state government operates its own bus service, private bus companies operate in the country as well. Like just about everything else in India, buses are often incredibly overcrowded. Passengers often ride on the roofs of buses if there is no room inside.

India also has its own airline, with two divisions. Indian Airlines covers domestic flights, while Air India carries passengers to other countries.

Other ways to travel in India include taxis, boats, and rickshaws. There is also a recently built underground subway in Kolkata, the only one in all of India.

Staying in Touch

Television is slowly catching on in the subcontinent. A 1999 census estimated that there are about 63 million televisions in the country, and about 562 television stations. Most upper- and middle-class households now own their own television sets. In small villages, televisions are often shared. If one family owns a television, it is normal for them to invite their neighbors—or even the whole village—over to watch it. They gather in the evenings to watch programs such as the nightly news or soap-opera-type dramas of popular religious stories.

India's telephone system has also improved in recent years, although connections can still be poor. Cellular phones are becoming popular among the middle classes.

The *Times of India* is the nation's most widespread English-language newspaper. The *Hindustan Times*, the *Indian Express*, and the *Statesman* are other newspapers popular among English speakers in India. There are also countless regional newspapers in all the major languages. Whether a person speaks Hindi, Malayalam, Oriya, or another language, he or she can read about what is happening in the world.

Who Lives in India?

ALMOST EVERYWHERE YOU GO IN INDIA, THERE ARE people. Even deep in the jungle or high on a lonely mountain-top, someone will come strolling along. India is the second most populated country in the world, with more than 15 percent of Earth's entire population. Only China has more people.

Opposite: **Schoolgirls**

Rising Numbers

The number of people in India recently hit 1 billion. In July 2000, the population was estimated at 1,014,003,817.

More than a billion people live in India.

There are many reasons for India's high population growth. Part of it is due to the importance of the family in India. All generations of a family usually live under one roof, from the tiniest babies to the oldest grandparents. Parents often rely on their children to take care of them in their old age. Due to disease, malnutrition, and accidents, some of these children may die early in life. This encourages parents to have many children, so they can be sure some of their children will live to be adults.

India's marriage customs are another reason for its high population growth. When a daughter marries, she leaves her family home and goes to live in the household of her new husband. Her parents can no longer rely on her to help with chores, bring in money, or take care of them when they age. Many Indian parents therefore prefer to have sons who will stay and help support the household. Some people will have many daughters before a son is finally born.

Population growth is also due to the slower rate at which people are dying. Health care in India has improved in recent years, with new vaccinations for diseases such as typhoid and polio. These deadly diseases used to kill many people. The average life expectancy in India is now about sixty-three years. Half a century ago, many people did not live past their fifties.

People are worried that the steady rise in population will cause shortages in food, housing, and employment. As early as 1952, a family-planning program was set up to help lower the birthrate. In many towns and villages, health centers are staffed with people who teach families about birth control and family planning. They believe that educating people about how to limit the size of their families will help slow the growth in population.

In some states, the birth rate is slowing down. In other places, however, most women are still having four or five children each. In fact, India's population has more than tripled since the beginning of the century.

India's Many Faces

People in India can be as diverse as their surroundings. From north to south and from east to west, Indians

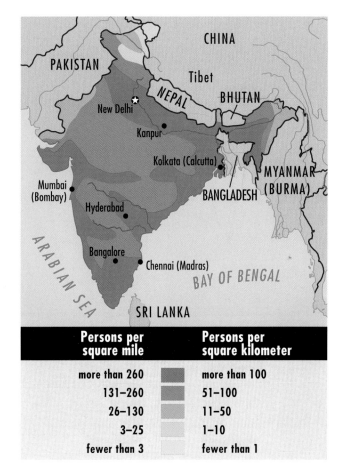

Persons per square mile		Persons per square kilometer
more than 260		more than 100
131–260		51–100
26–130		11–50
3–25		1–10
fewer than 3		fewer than 1

These Kashmiri shepherds and merchant reflect some of the diverse faces of India.

often vary in their height, skin color, and facial features. Their faces reflect the centuries of migration from all over the world to the Indian subcontinent.

About 72 percent of all Indians are Indo-Aryans. They are the descendants of the early Aryan invaders who mixed with

Young women of Gujarat

Dravidians usually have much darker skin than other Indians.

the people of the Indus Valley. Indo-Aryans live mostly in northwestern and central India and are often a little taller and lighter-skinned than the Indians in the far south.

Most southern Indians are Dravidians. Their ancestors were the original Dravidians of the south and the people of the Indus Valley who did not mix with the Aryans but rather moved south to merge their culture with that of the Dravidians. Modern Dravidians are often shorter than the people in the north, and their skin is usually much darker, sometimes almost black. They make up about 25 percent of the population.

Who Lives in India?

Indo-Aryan	72%
Dravidian	25%
Mongoloid and other	3%

The remaining 3 percent of Indians are Mongoloids. These people resemble Asians to the north and east of India. They have lighter skin, rounder faces, and more slanted eyes. They come from countries such as Nepal, Bhutan, and Myanmar. Many of them are refugees from Tibet who have chosen to settle in India rather than live in their own Chinese-occupied country. Most Mongoloids live in the Himalayan region and in the northeastern state of Assam.

This Mongoloid girl lives in Sikkim.

A festive gathering
of Adivasis

Adivasis

About 7.5 percent of India's people belong to various tribes. They are commonly known as *Adivasis*, and they live mostly in the forests and rural areas in eastern and central India. About 400 tribal groups exist in India. These tribes try to live by their own rules and follow their own customs.

Adivasis often live unsettled lives. Many of their homes are threatened by modern technology. Their forests are often cut down for lumber or cleared to build mines. In some places, their homes have been flooded by irrigation projects such as hydro-electric dams. The destruction of their way of life has made many Adivasis angry. In protest, some Adivasis in one part of India are urging the Indian government to grant them their own state.

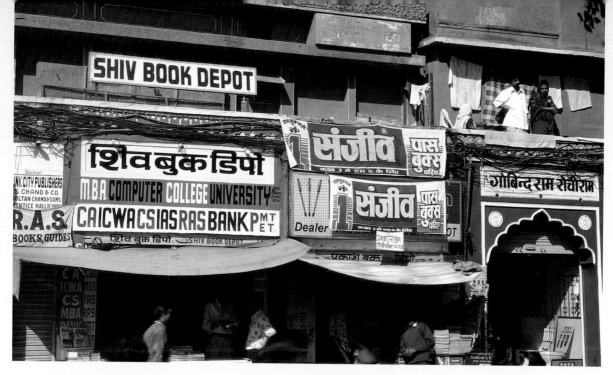

The Hindi Alphabet

Hindi is written in the Devanagari script, which evolved in north India through many centuries. Like English, it is written from left to right. The Hindi alphabet has 46 basic characters: 35 consonants and 11 vowels. Unlike English, most of these characters represent only one sound. Therefore, with very few exceptions, what is written is how it is pronounced. Hindi is spoken mainly in the states of Uttar Pradesh, Madhya Pradesh, Bihar, and Rajasthan.

Languages and Dialects

Most countries have a single language that is spoken by the majority of its citizens. In India, however, the government recognizes fifteen official languages. In addition to the official languages, more than 700 dialects are spoken in India.

The official languages can be broken into two groups. The languages found in south India are called the Dravidian languages. They originated from the languages spoken by the first inhabitants of India. The Dravidian languages are Tamil, Malayalam, Telugu, and Kannada. They use a different alphabet from the languages in the north.

Most of the northern languages come from Sanskrit, which was used by the scholars and nobles in ancient Indo-Aryan culture. But even though they sprang from the same language and have similar alphabets, each of the modern northern languages can sound very different. For instance, a Hindi speaker can have a lot of trouble understanding someone who speaks only Bengali. The official northern languages are Hindi, Bengali, Marathi, Urdu, Gujarati, Oriya, Punjabi, Kashmiri, Sindhi, Sanskrit, and Assamese.

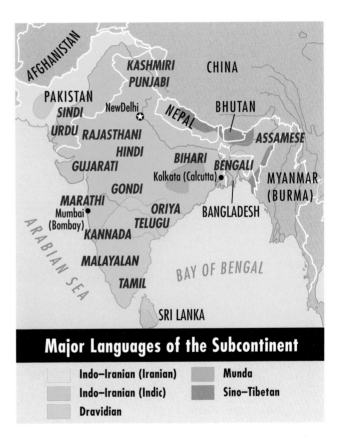

Major Languages of the Subcontinent

Indo–Iranian (Iranian)
Indo–Iranian (Indic)
Dravidian
Munda
Sino–Tibetan

In an effort to draw Indians together after independence, the Indian government proclaimed Hindi the national language. People still protest this adoption, however, since many Indians do not speak or understand Hindi. South Indians are especially upset because their languages are completely different from Hindi.

Because Indians from different parts of the country can have so much trouble understanding each other, English is commonly used to bridge the gap. In government schools, both Hindi and English are usually taught in addition to the dialect commonly spoken in that particular region.

City Problems

Life in an Indian city can be very difficult. Because the cities are so crowded, it is often hard to find decent places to live or even enough to eat. Each year, more and more people move to the cities from rural areas. If droughts or floods destroy their farms, many farmers move to the nearest city in search of work. However, there are few jobs in the cities, and these people often have to sleep on the streets.

Population of Major Cities (2000 est.)

Mumbai (Bombay)	15 million
Kolkata (Calcutta)	12 million
Delhi	11.3 million
Chennai (Madras)	5.9 million
Bangalore	5.2 million

Homelessness is a huge problem in Indian cities. Most of the people without homes are immigrants from rural areas, but many are also orphaned children with nowhere else to go. They must do all their daily tasks on the street, from cooking to bathing. Sometimes they beg for money to live or collect rags and other junk to sell. Some people have more stable jobs, such as pulling a rickshaw. After a long, hard day of working, they return at night to the small patch of pavement that they call home.

If they save enough money, a homeless family can rent a small space in a slum. Although they provide some shelter, slums in Indian cities are often not much more comfortable than the streets. In these slums, a whole family must share a tiny shack made of rags, wooden boards, and scraps of metal, with no electricity or running water. Open sewers often run right past their doors, and disease epidemics are common.

Most cities in India have slums. People build shacks in vacant lots or on empty stretches of pavement. Sometimes there are makeshift homes even in the central business districts of Delhi and Kolkata. Some of Asia's largest slums are found in the congested streets of Mumbai.

Children living in makeshift homes alongside train tracks in Kolkata

Temples, Mosques, and Gurdwaras

FOR MOST INDIANS, RELIGION IS AS IMPORTANT AS EATING and sleeping. Its influence is seen everywhere, from Muslims touching their heads to the ground during their morning prayers to women leaving offerings of flowers and sweets at a Hindu shrine. Most Indians live their lives by the rules of their religion. An Indian's chosen religion tells him or her how to dress, eat, bathe, and act toward others.

India is home to some of the world's most important religions. Some of them, such as Buddhism, began in India and

Opposite: **A Hindu temple beside a lake**

Colorful prayer flags at a Buddhist monastery

spread all over the world. Others, such as Islam and Christianity, were brought to India by visitors or invading armies. Two religions, Jainism and Sikhism, are practiced mostly in India. The nation's main religion, Hinduism, began to evolve almost 4,000 years ago and is now a basic element of Indian culture.

Hinduism

Hinduism is the most widely practiced religion in India. About 80 percent of the population call themselves Hindu. Two of the most important founders of independent India, Mahatma Gandhi and Jawaharlal Nehru, were Hindus.

Some Important Hindu Holidays

Holi (February or March): The celebration of the end of winter and the beginning of spring. Huge bonfires are lit the night before to commemorate the goddess Holika. On the day of Holi, people celebrate by dancing, singing, and throwing colored water and powder at each other. The different colors symbolize the many colors of spring.

Diwali/Deepavali (October or November): Also known as the Festival of Lights and the Festival of Sweets. It lasts five days, beginning with people cleaning and decorating their houses and themselves. At night, oil lamps are lit everywhere to help the god Rama find his way home. Celebrators give each other

sweets, and on the fifth day, sisters paint a mark of respect on their brothers' foreheads.

Hinduism began when the Aryan invaders mingled their beliefs with those belonging to the Indus Valley people and the Dravidians in the south. The basic teachings of Hinduism were recorded sometime between 1500 and 1000 B.C., in written scriptures called the Vedas. As the religion grew, more holy books were written. The four Vedas are the most important of these books. They describe the basic philosophy of Hinduism. The Upanishads are included within the Vedas and discuss the nature of the universe and the soul.

The Mahabharata is also an important Hindu holy book. It is an epic poem of more than 220,000 lines that describes the lives, wars, and adventures of the Hindu gods and their human worshipers. One aspect of this poem that is especially

An image of Shiva dancing

loved by Hindus is the Bhagavad Gita, in which the god Krishna explains his philosophies to Prince Arjuna. The Ramayana is another. It tells the story about how the Hindu god Rama rescued his wife, Sita, from the demon Ravanna.

Similar to Christians and Jews, Hindus believe that there is one Supreme Force in the universe. However, in Hinduism this force is split into many smaller gods to help people understand the many different parts of life.

In modern Hinduism, there are three main gods. They are Brahma, the creator of the universe; Vishnu, who preserves it; and Shiva, who destroys it. This cycle then repeats, again and again.

Sri Ramakrishna

Born in 1836, Sri Ramakrishna was a Hindu religious teacher and spiritual guide. He lived in a small room in the Dakshineswar temple garden on the outskirts of Kolkata, where he received his visitors and disciples. Ramakrishna taught that all religions are basically the same, and that people from different religions should live together in harmony. He said, "As many faiths, so many paths." Ramakrishna inspired a huge following. Many religious centers now teach his beliefs. One of his followers, Swami Vivekananda, helped spread Hinduism to people around the world.

Some of the Hindu goddesses are Lakshmi, the goddess of wealth; Sarasvati, the goddess of music and learning; and Shiva's wife, Parvati. Parvati often doubles as Durga, the killer of ignorance, and as Kali, who reminds people of the forces of life and death. These are only a few of the Hindu gods, however. Traditionally, there are about 330 million gods and demons in Hinduism.

Hindus believe in reincarnation, the idea that when they die, their souls are reborn in another living creature. Two other important ideas, *karma* and *dharma*, are related to this belief. Karma can be defined as a record of a person's good and bad deeds. If a person dies with bad karma, he or she will most likely be reborn in a lowly form, such as a worm or a beetle. If the person dies with good karma, however, the next life is sure to be better. In order to gain good karma, a Hindu has to perform his or her dharma. Dharma can be defined as the group of moral duties that belong to each living creature. For example, a priest must perform religious services, and a housewife must cook and clean. If people perform their dharma well, they gain good kharma and are therefore reborn into a better life after they die.

The final goal for Hindus is *moksha*, or spiritual salvation. If they gain enough good karma, they will eventually reach moksha, escaping the cycle of death and rebirth.

The rules of dharma order the lives of devout Hindus, even when it comes to food. Since it is considered wrong to eat animals, many Hindus are vegetarians. Also, in Hinduism cows are sacred, so very few practicing Hindus will eat beef. Cleanliness is also very important. Most Hindus bathe every day if they can. To gain good karma, it is also customary for Hindus to perform regular *pujas*, which are special rituals that show appreciation for the gods. During a puja, a Hindu lights candles, burns incense, chants, and leaves offerings of food and flowers at an image of a god.

One city is especially holy to Hindus. This is Varanasi, or Benares, in the northern state of Uttar Pradesh. Hindus

Pilgrims bathing in the Ganges River

believe that if they die in Varanasi and are cremated on the banks of the holy Ganges River, their souls will immediately attain moksha. Hindus believe that the Ganges River is holy because it flowed down from the god Shiva's hair. Many pilgrims visit Varanasi and other cities along the Ganges, to die and achieve salvation or just to bathe in the river's holy waters.

Even though only about 14 percent of India's population practices Islam, the nation still has the second-largest number of Muslims in the world. Islam came to the subcontinent in the eighth century. It was later spread by the Mughals, who ruled northern India from 1526 to the 1700s.

Islam was founded in A.D. 610 by an Arab named Muhammad. Muhammad had a vision that there is only one god, whose name is Allah. To convert to Islam, a person only has to say, "There is no god but Allah, and Muhammad is his prophet." Muhammad's teachings are collected in a holy book called the Koran, which is read and followed by Muslims all over the world.

Muslims believe that God cannot be worshiped as an idol. They do not use statues or idols in their religion. Instead, they pray at least five times a day facing Mecca, where Muhammad

Muslims praying at Delhi's huge mosque, the Jama Masjid

was born. Many Muslims try to make a pilgrimage to Mecca at least once in their lifetimes. Muslim temples, called *mosques*, are often crowded before sunrise and after sunset with devotees coming to pray. The man who calls people to prayers is called the *muezzin*. He stands at the top of the mosque, in a tower called a *minaret*. His wavering, melodic call can sound very beautiful drifting over the rooftops after sunset or before sunrise.

The Koran is very similar to the Old Testament, which is followed by Jews and Christians. In fact, Muslims accept both Moses and Jesus as Muslim prophets. Islam preaches ideas that are similar to both Christianity and Judaism, including piety and goodwill toward one's neighbors. Most Muslims do not drink alcohol or eat pork, because pigs are considered unclean. As in Hinduism, cleanliness is important. Water tanks are located outside most mosques where Muslims wash their feet before going inside to pray.

Some Indian Muslims stayed in India after Partition. Many Muslims, however, moved to Pakistan.

Buddhism

About 2,500 years ago, a Hindu prince named Siddhartha Gautama was born in the Himalayan foothills. He grew up to be a skilled athlete and scholar, enjoying the rich life of a prince. When he was twenty-nine, Siddhartha began to think about mortality. He grew tired and unhappy with his wealth. He gave it all up and went into the forest to fast and pray. After starving himself for a long time, he found that that was not the key to spiritual understanding. He meditated for many more days, until he began to look at the world in a new way. This new way of thinking was called his Enlightenment. As an Enlightened Being, Siddhartha was now known as a Buddha. He began to travel around India, preaching his new ideas.

This collection of ideas, which came to be known as Buddhism, is more of a philosophy than a religion. Buddhists do not pray to a god but rather look within themselves for the truth. They try to follow the Middle Way taught by the Buddha. Instead of living in extremes such as being very rich or very poor, Buddhists try to live somewhere in the middle. The goal of all Buddhists is *nirvana*, a spiritual peace that is similar to the Hindu moksha. Buddhists also believe in karma, the effect of their good and bad deeds on their next lives. They believe that if they rid themselves of all their worldly desires, they will not suffer anymore and will eventually reach the utter peace of nirvana.

Although Buddhism was born in India, now it is practiced by only a small part of the population. Despite its small following in India, Buddhism is the fourth-largest religion in the world. Over the centuries, it has spread all over Asia. In India, many low-caste Hindus have become Buddhists in order to escape the caste system. Many people in western nations have also embraced the Buddhist philosophy.

Most Buddhist monks begin studying when they are very young. In areas where Buddhism is practiced, young boys are sent to monasteries to learn the teachings of the Buddha.

Young Buddhist monks

In India, most of these monasteries are found in the Himalayan foothills, especially in Ladakh and the states of Sikkim and Himachal Pradesh.

Sikhism

Sikhism is a religion unique to India. It was founded in the sixteenth century by a man who came to be known as Guru Nanak. He lived in the Punjab, an area where many Hindus and Muslims lived. He began Sikhism in an effort to combine the best of Hinduism and Islam. The term *sikh* comes from a Sanskrit word meaning "disciple."

A Sikh man

Like Muslims, Sikhs believe in only one god and reject the caste system. However, many of their customs are similar to Hindu customs. They cremate their dead, and they also believe in rebirth and the importance of karma. In fact, the two religions have so many similarities that marriage between a Sikh and a Hindu is common.

In the eighteenth century, a man named Guru Gobind Singh began to teach Sikhs how to be strong warriors. He wanted Sikhs to be able to protect themselves against the Muslims who were oppressing them. Because of this part of Sikhism, many Sikhs now have reputations as warriors.

Sikh men can easily be spotted in a crowd due to certain symbols introduced by Guru Gobind Singh. The most obvious is their hair, which they are not allowed to cut. Sikh men twist their long hair up into turbans and often braid their beards. Other symbols worn by many Sikhs are a wooden or ivory comb (symbol of cleanliness), shorts called *kuccha* (symbol of alertness), a steel bracelet (symbol of determination), and a sword called a *kirpan*, which is used for the defense of the weak.

Sikhism had ten *gurus*, or religious teachers, including Guru Nanak and Guru Gobind Singh. Their teachings were collected in the Granth Sahib, which is now the Sikh holy book. It includes many Hindu and Muslim teachings.

There are about 18 million Sikhs in India today, most of whom live in Punjab. Sikhs practice love, hospitality, and tolerance of others. They will welcome anybody into their temples, which are called *gurdwaras*. The holiest gurdwara is the Golden Temple in Amritsar. It is made of bronze plates covered in pure gold leaf. Most Sikhs try to visit it at least once in their lifetime.

Jainism

Jainism was founded around 500 B.C., about the same time that Buddhism developed. A Hindu named Vardhamana was born to a wealthy and important family in north India. When Vardhamana was thirty years old, his parents died. After this, he became an ascetic, someone who gives up all worldly possessions to spend his life in search of spiritual understanding. Vardhamana wandered through India for twelve years as an ascetic. He slowly formed a series of ideas that he began to preach to others. This group of beliefs became the basics of Jainism.

Jains share some Hindu beliefs, such as karma and reincarnation. However, they do not accept the caste system or the belief in gods. Similar to Buddhists, Jains search within themselves for understanding of the spiritual world. To attain eternal peace, Jains strive to rid themselves of all earthly desires and to practice love for all living creatures.

One of the most important aspects of Jainism is *ahimsa* (nonviolence). Jains refuse to kill any other living animals. Most Jains are strict vegetarians. Some sweep the streets in front of them as they walk so that they will not step on any living creatures. Some Jain monks even wear cloth masks to avoid breathing in any insects by mistake.

Jains make up only about 0.5 percent of the population. However, their temples can be found in many parts of India, mostly in the west and the southwest. Jain temples are usually very ornate, filled with beautifully carved sculptures and columns.

Zoroastrianism

Zoroastrianism is one of the oldest religions in the world. Its influence used to stretch all the way from India to the Mediterranean. Now it is practiced mainly in three places— Shiraz in Iran, Karachi in Pakistan, and Mumbai in India.

This religion began in the sixth or seventh century B.C. with the prophet Zarathustra, who is also called Zoroaster. The holy book of Zoroastrianism is called the Zend-Avesta.

Their god is Ahura Mazda, who is symbolized by fire. To honor him, followers always keep fires burning in their temples.

In India, followers of this religion are called Parsis. They try to triumph over evil by practicing three rules—*humata* (good thoughts), *hukta* (good words), and *huvarshta* (good deeds). They believe that the elements of fire, earth, water, and air should not be polluted. To avoid this, Parsis do not bury or cremate their dead. Instead, they leave the bodies in buildings called Towers of Silence, to be picked clean by vultures.

Only about 85,000 Parsis live in India today. They are a strong influence in Mumbai and have many communities throughout the city.

Major Religions of India	
Hinduism	80%
Islam	14%
Christianity	2.4%
Sikhism	2%
Buddhism	0.7%
Jainism	0.5%
Other	0.4%

Judaism and Christianity

The largest and oldest Jewish community in India is in the city of Kochi (formerly Cochin) in Kerala. The first Jews probably came to Kochi as early as 587 B.C.

Almost 3 percent of India's population is Christian. Although Christians are scattered throughout the country, most live in Kerala and Goa. Some people believe that one of Jesus' apostles, Saint Thomas, came to India in A.D. 52.

Christian children receiving religious instruction

Music,
Movies, and
Sports

On any day, take a look at a street in an Indian town. A crowd gathers outside a movie theater, eagerly waiting to see that week's most popular movie. Across the street a shop sells hand-carved figurines of Hindu gods. The window of another shop displays the newest Indian novels next to ancient religious texts. A group of boys play a noisy game of cricket on the corner, while women in handwoven saris weave gracefully through the crowd. Some of the buildings have arched, filigreed doorways from Mughal times while others are Hindu temples decorated with colorful statues of the gods.

Indian culture reflects the country's oldest traditions side by side with its newest developments. India's literature, films, architecture, and sports are as varied and complicated as everything else in the country.

Opposite: **A musician accompanies a traditional dancer.**

A cricket match

Sports and Hobbies

Cricket is probably the most popular sport in India. Introduced by the British, it is now part of the lives of most Indians. Almost every Indian either plays or watches cricket.

Cricket grounds are found just about everywhere in India. Whether it is an alley in Kolkata, on a formal playing field in Mumbai, or even on the steps by the

Ganges River in Varanasi, chances are that people will gather there at some point for a noisy and competitive game of cricket. India's national cricket team is one of the largest and most skilled in the world. It plays regularly against the teams of such countries as Australia, South Africa, Pakistan, and England.

Other popular sports in India are soccer, basketball, volleyball, and polo. Hockey is considered the national sport. The first time India's hockey team won the Olympic Games was in 1928. Since then, the team has had victories over the teams of such countries as England, the Netherlands, and Germany. The Indian hockey team has won medals in the Olympic Games five times.

In many Indian villages, people still compete in a traditional wrestling sport called *kabaddi*. This game is most popular with younger and adolescent boys. Kite flying is also a fun hobby for many Indians, from small children to old men and women. When the breeze is right, people launch their colorful kites into the sky and watch them float over rooftops, beaches, or open fields.

Music, Dance, and Drama

Few things are more beloved in India than music. Singing is a part of daily life, from morning prayers to children's lullabies at night. Much of India's music stems from its religions. During their religious rituals, Hindus chant songs called *ragas* to please the gods. For Muslims, the muezzin's daily call to prayer is a beautiful melody that drifts over the rooftops after sunset and just before dawn.

Indian classical music has become famous for its unique sounds. A stringed instrument called a *sitar* is often combined with a pair of drums called *tablas* and a wooden flute to create music that is the essence of India for many people. While a lot of music lovers listen only to the recordings, some also attend live concerts to enjoy the classical music up close.

Most Indian dance is an expression of religious devotion. Classical Hindu dancers use their bodies to tell the stories of gods such as Shiva, Parvati, and Rama. Although these dances are quick and energetic, each movement has its own meaning based on Hindu myths.

Ravi Shankar

Born in 1920, Ravi Shankar is famous for composing and playing classical Indian music. His specialty is the sitar. Ravi Shankar was especially popular in the United States during the 1960s and is credited with bringing Indian music to the Western world. He has written two concertos and numerous ballet and film scores, and he has worked with many famous musicians such as Philip Glass and former Beatle George Harrison.

The four basic types of classical dance are *Bharata Natyam*, *Manipuri*, *Kathak*, and *Kathakali*. Bharata Natyam is a very popular but difficult type of dance. Its dancers are usually women, who are never allowed to dance upright but must always keep their knees bent. Manipuri comes from the Manipur region in northeastern India. It is noted for the conical caps and hoop skirts worn by its dancers. Kathak dancers wear ankle bells and dance straight-legged. Their costumes are often similar to those shown in ancient Mughal paintings.

Bharata Natyam is a difficult dance form.

Kathakali is widespread in Kerala and is famous for the complex costumes of its dancers. A Kathakali dancer spends at least an hour donning his costume and applying his makeup, while the actual performance usually lasts for about ten to twelve hours!

There are also countless folk dances throughout India that have existed for centuries. These dances range from the religious dances of the Buddhist monks to the ankle-bell-jangling performances in Rajasthan. In Tamil Nadu, agile folk dancers perform the *Koklikatai* raised high on stilts.

A scene from a dramatization of the Ramayana

Like both its music and its dance, much of India's drama developed from religious beliefs. A common form of entertainment in villages is to gather around a small, makeshift stage to watch actors present the beloved story of the Ramayana. Most Indians watch this drama at least once. Popular religious plays are also acted out in the larger cities. Many have even been adapted for television, so that Indians can watch the antics of the gods in their own homes.

Literature

Indian literature can be traced back nearly 3,000 years. The first Hindu scriptures, the Vedas, make up one of the earliest bodies of literature in the world. Later Hindu writings continued this tradition and are still read widely today. The Mahabharata is one of India's greatest literary successes.

The holy books of both the Sikhs and the Jains were also written in India. Since then, many writers and storytellers have added to and rephrased these stories, keeping them alive throughout the years. Hindu writers especially enjoy retelling the tales of the gods in new and exciting ways.

Around the beginning of the twentieth century, more Indian writers began to write stories and novels. One of these was the beloved poet and writer Rabindranath Tagore, who wrote many stories about life in rural Bengal. R. K. Narayan was another twentieth-century writer. Most of his stories are set in South India, in a fictional town called Malgudi. The works of both of these writers are still very popular today.

Rabindranath Tagore

Born in Bengal in 1861, Rabindranath Tagore is considered the national poet of India. Not only did he compose the national anthem, he also wrote many stories and poems that have become pillars of Indian culture. The university that he founded at Shantiniketan has educated some of the most important people in India. In 1913, Tagore won the Nobel Prize for Literature. Tagore was also active in the Independence Movement. He was knighted by the British in 1915 but returned that honor in 1919 to protest the Amritsar Massacre. Most of Tagore's writing is set in his native Bengal, bringing to life the people, land, and culture of that region. He died in 1941.

More women writers emerged during the twentieth century. Mahasweta Devi, Gita Mehta, and Kamala Markandaya are only a few. Their stories, especially Markandaya's *Nectar in a Sieve* and Gita Mehta's *Raj*, tell what life is like for women in India.

Many Indian authors write in Indian languages, such as Hindi, Bengali, and Tamil. However, some writers have begun to write in English as well. These writers include Vikram Seth (*A Suitable Boy*), Salman Rushdie (*Midnight's Children* and *The Moor's Last Sigh*), and Anita Desai (*Clear Light of Day* and *In Custody*). Other contemporary Indian writers are Amitav Ghosh, Bharati Mukherjee, Bapsi Sidhwa, and Rohinton Mistry, whose novel, *A Fine Balance*, is already considered a classic.

Khajuraho temple carvings

Painting and Sculpture

Even if you wanted to, it would be hard to avoid art in India. There are paintings, frescoes, and sculptures in almost every Indian town. Most of them are religious, and they are found both inside and outside of temples.

Although Muslim invaders knocked down many ancient Hindu temples, some still stand. Khajuraho is one of the most famous temple sites. The temples there are carved inside and out with complex figures of people going about their daily life. Mahabalipuram, in the south, is another town famous for its sculptors. The chinking of chisels against stone is heard from dawn to dusk, as sculptors carve statues that will be used in homes and temples all over India.

Some of India's oldest and most beautiful art is found at Ajanta and Ellora in the state of Maharashtra. At both places, there are a number of large caves that Buddhists filled long ago with sculptures and frescoes. The figures were carved out of the hills themselves, creating caves whose walls are lined with carvings of the Buddha's life and teachings.

In addition to India's history of art, many Indians paint and sculpt today. While some continue creating religious art, many have branched out in different directions. The work of India's contemporary artists is found in modern art museums and galleries in most of its big cities, such as the Academy of Fine Arts in Kolkata.

Ancient Ruins and Modern Buildings

Ruins, the remains of ancient kingdoms, dot the Indian countryside. One of the largest collection of ruins is at Hampi in the state of Karnataka. With a circumference of about 12.5 miles (20 km), this vast stretch of fallen temples and palaces displays the last traces of the Vijayanagar Empire. Members of that empire built buildings so secure that they still exist more than 600 years later.

The Mughal invaders in the north brought their own building style. Mughal buildings are distinguished by their arched doorways and windows, minarets, domes, and elaborate decorations carved on the marble walls and covered in gemstones. In Delhi, the Mughals built the Red Fort, Jama Masjid, and many other buildings that are still used. In Agra, the most famous Mughal structure is the Taj Mahal, completed by Shah Jahan in 1653.

The British also left their mark on Indian architecture. The Victoria Memorial in Kolkata is one of the largest examples of British architecture in India. It was built for Queen Victoria in the early 1900s.

A number of palaces remain from the days of Indian princes. One of the largest is in Mysore. It features marble floors, gold filigree, arched doorways, and wide, smooth steps.

Detail of the elaborate stonework decorating the Taj Mahal

Local Crafts

Even though the number of factories is increasing, most goods in India are made by hand. People make crafts in their homes or in shops where they also sell their goods. India is one of the largest and most famous producers of handicrafts in the world.

Most Indian textiles are still woven by hand. Silk is the most popular fabric created in Varanasi, while Kashmir is famous for its rich woolen and cotton shawls. In Rajasthan, men weave colorful cloth and women decorate it with beads and mirrors to create clothes and hangings that flash in the sun.

Carving a small statue from wood

Indian carpets are some of the most beautiful in the world, especially those made in Kashmir. Carpet weavers often use designs that were brought from Persia hundreds of years ago.

Indian artisans are also experts at making cups, bowls, jewelry boxes, trays, and candlesticks. In Kashmir, they make such goods out of papier-mâche and Indian walnut. In Rajasthan, these objects are either pottery or copper and brass inlaid with colorful enamel. In the south, people use rosewood and teak to fashion furniture such as tables, chairs, and cupboards.

Indian craftspeople also dedicate their time to creating figurines and small statues. Most of these represent Hindu gods or elephants and other animals. They are made out of metal or wood, or are chiseled expertly out of stone.

Satyajit Ray

Satyajit Ray was one of India's first serious filmmakers. He was born in 1921. In 1947, he helped found Calcutta's first film society, which still exists today. His first film, *Pather Panchali* (*Song of the Little Road*), won several international awards and brought him worldwide fame. He went on to write, direct, and produce about twenty-eight more films, many of which are set to music that he composed. Ray's films concern everyday human problems, and most of them are set in small Bengali villages or Indian cities.

One of the most popular forms of entertainment in India is going to the cinema. About 5 billion movie tickets are sold in India each year. Movies are advertised on huge, colorful billboards, often painted by hand. Movie soundtracks are played everywhere—in homes, in restaurants, even in buses hurtling through dusty towns at night.

The Indian film industry produces more than 1,000 movies a year, more than any other film industry in the world. Mumbai and Chennai are the largest movie producers in India, followed closely by Kolkata.

Popular Indian movies are a mixture of romance, family feuds, and crime, all set to an energetic soundtrack. Most movies are musicals, with the actors constantly breaking into songs and complex dance routines. Many people think a movie is a failure if there are not enough songs.

Billboards advertising Indian movies

India's movie industry also produces more serious films. One film director, Satyajit Ray, won a Lifetime Achievement Award for his work. Other famous film directors are Mrinal Sen and Raj Kapoor. A more recent director is Deepa Mehta, whose films *Fire* and *Earth* have won international acclaim.

Daily
Routines

THE DAY BEGINS AT DAWN FOR MOST INDIANS. DURING THE hot season, this is the only time cool enough to get things done. In the blue hours just before sunrise, people get up, get dressed, and eat breakfast. Most Indians bathe every day if they can. In many places, they cluster around communal water pumps for quick baths before the day begins.

During the morning, people go about their daily activities. Some people travel to their jobs in shops, banks, or offices. Others work in the fields. Some stay at home to cook, mend, and clean. Before they begin, however, many Indians pay a visit to a temple or shrine of their religion to show respect for the gods.

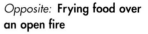

Opposite: **Frying food over an open fire**

National Holidays in India

New Year's Day	January 1
Republic Day	January 26
Independence Day	August 15
Mahatma Gandhi's Birthday	October 2

Pilgrims offer their morning prayers.

A boy at work in a South Indian field

After the midday meal is eaten, some people return to their work. During the hottest weeks of summer, many people prefer to stay inside during the afternoon. They rest or sleep in the cool shade, waiting until the hottest hours have passed. Once the sun's heat lessens, people go out, and the streets come alive again.

In India, most people go to bed early. By ten o'clock, the streets are usually quiet, except for a thin trickle of traffic. Then the long, dusty Indian night begins, stretching out until the sun's first light signals the start of another day.

Family Life and Marriage

Family members of all ages usually live together under one roof, from the oldest grandmother to the smallest newborn. The eldest man is considered the head of the household, but the older women often have a lot to say, too. Everyone in the family shares the chores, even the children. Women usually cook and clean and often help the men working in the fields as well. Children help however they can, whether by collecting wood and dung for fuel or by leading the family's buffalo herd into the river for its afternoon bath.

Hindu Weddings

Traditional Hindu weddings are very long and festive affairs. The bridegroom usually arrives at the ceremony wearing a turban and sitting on a white horse. The bride wears a red sari and gold jewelry. She paints intricate patterns with henna on her palms and the soles of her feet. During the all-day affair, guests eat, drink, play music, and dance. A priest counsels the bride and the groom about their duties during marriage. After he places a colorful mark called a *tika* on their foreheads, they circle a sacred fire seven times before they are pronounced husband and wife. After the wedding is over, the bride often goes to live with her husband's family.

When a man marries, he brings his new bride into his family's home. In many places, it is common for a bride to bring a dowry to her new husband's family. This is a collection of gifts

Traditional Clothing

Most Indian women wear *saris* or *salwaar-kameez*. Saris are long, wide lengths of cloth that are wrapped expertly around a woman's body to create a skirt and shoulder covering. Underneath their saris, women wear petticoats and short, tight blouses called *cholis*. Another popular outfit for women is the salwaar-kameez. Salwaars are loose trousers worn under the long, loose tunic called a kameez.

Many Indian men wear loose shirts called *kurtas* with either *dhotis* or *lungis*. A dhoti is a length of cloth wrapped around the waist with a separate length pulled up between the legs. Lungis are wide rectangles of cloth wrapped around the waist and either left hanging to the ground or rolled up to leave the legs free.

and money to help her and her new family. This tradition is often criticized, because it is hard for poor families to come up with a dowry. Many families go into debt just from marrying off their daughters. A lot of parents do not want daughters, because they will cost them so much money when they marry. Some people are trying to abolish dowries so that daughters will be as welcome as sons when they are born.

In traditional India, parents usually arrange their children's marriages. Parents search for mates for their children either through people they know or in classified advertisements in newspapers. Once they have found somebody suitable, they arrange a meeting between the two young people. If they like each other, the boy and the girl will usually consent to marriage. If they do not get along, however, the parents keep looking until they find a good match.

This tradition is still widely practiced in India, especially in the villages. It is changing in some places, however, mostly in the larger cities. Young people now go out on dates more, and they often choose their own husbands or wives without the help of their parents.

Education

In a country with so many people, it is difficult to build enough schools for all the children. Many children still do not go to school at all or stop when they are still very young in order to work. For the children who go to school, supplies such as textbooks are often scarce. Because of these problems, about half of India's population still cannot read or write.

Village schoolchildren writing on slates

Village schools are usually very small and simple. Children often sit outside to study lessons, either on the ground or on benches. Many still use slates and chalk to write because paper and pencils are hard to get. Schools in larger towns and cities usually have their own buildings with indoor classrooms, as well as special uniforms for their students.

More Indians go to college now than ever before. There are about 130 universities in India plus a number of smaller colleges.

College students socializing between classes

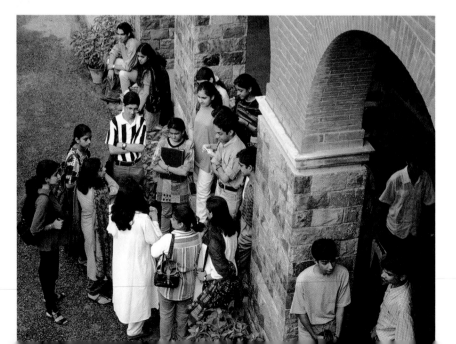

When a Hindu dies in India, it is customary to burn, or cremate, the body. The body is placed on a wooden pyre and sprinkled with rose water and sandalwood paste before it is burnt. Afterward, the ashes are scattered to the winds or thrown into a holy river. Indians show their grief by shaving their heads and wearing white, the color of mourning. Muslims and Christians are usually buried.

Home Sweet Home

Most Indian houses are fairly small and simple. In villages, houses are usually made out of mud mixed with straw. The walls are thick and sturdy to keep the interiors cool in the summer and warm in the winter. Roofs are usually thatched with straw or, if the family can afford it, tiled with slate. The windows have no glass, but in larger houses they are usually screened with metal grates to keep out intruders. Many houses have inner courtyards that are useful as cooking spaces or as places to hang laundry.

A house in rural West Bengal

Indians usually sleep and live in the same room. During the day, bedding is rolled up and beds leaned against the walls to make room for daily activities. When it is very hot, most people sleep outside in their yards or on top of their roofs.

The Caste System

For thousands of years, Hindu society has been organized into levels according to the caste system. Each level was first determined by the occupations of its members, but later, people were born into their parents' caste. It was begun by the Aryans and later supported by the British. The original, darker-skinned people were at the bottom of the caste sytem. As time went on, this system became more rigid. Aryan priests (*Brahmans*) established themselves at the top. Next came the rulers and warriors (*Kshatriyas*), then the farmers and merchants (*Vaisyas*) and the servants and slaves (*Sudras*). At the very bottom of the pyramid were the "untouchables" or outcastes (more recently called Dalits), people whose jobs were considered so unclean that they could not even be touched.

Because this system led to prejudice and separation among people, it was abolished in 1950. However, some people still choose to follow it.

In cities, most people live in similar houses, although these are usually built out of wood and plaster. Many people also live in apartment buildings. These range from the glossy high-rises of the rich to the cramped, crowded homes of the poor. Some people even sleep where they work, whether on the floors of shops or sprawled out on the seat of a rickshaw.

Due to the shortage of money and housing, many Indians also live in slums. Slum houses are usually makeshift one-room shacks made out of metal, rags, scraps of wood, and anything else that can be found. In these slums, electricity and safe drinking water are hard to find.

Spices and Sweets

Indian food is famous for its many spicy flavors and strong aromas. When they came to India, the British were overwhelmed by all the spicy foods that they discovered. To simplify it for themselves, they called it all "curry." In fact, in India there is no such thing as curry. Indian cooks use many different spices in their kitchens, to create a variety of dishes. Some of the more popular spices are cumin, turmeric, chilies, coriander, ginger, saffron, mustard, pepper, and garlic.

Rice is the basic food of most Indians. *Dahl*, a sauce made out of lentils, is usually poured on top of the rice. Some people eat just rice and dahl, while others combine it with meat

A mother feeds her daughter.

or vegetables that have been cooked with various spices. While most Indians are vegetarians, some eat lamb, chicken, mutton, or even beef. Vegetarian dishes are different combinations of potatoes, peas, cauliflower, okra, tomatoes, chickpeas, and eggplant.

The different spices in each dish give it its distinctive flavor. A northern favorite is *tandoori* chicken. Cooks make this by soaking the chicken in a yogurt-and-spice sauce before baking it in a clay oven called a *tandoor*.

People often eat these dishes with different kinds of bread. Most Indian breads are unleavened and cooked like pancakes on hot plates. A southern specialty is the *masala dosa*, which is a rice-flour pancake rolled around spiced potatoes and onions and served with dahl and coconut chutney.

Most Indians enjoy sweets, too. *Ras gullas*, cream-cheese balls flavored with rose water, are one favorite dessert. There is also *kulfi*, a kind of ice cream, and *jalebis*, which are orange-colored squiggles filled with syrup. Sweets are made for special occasions, given as gifts, or left as offerings at religious shrines.

To quench their thirst, a lot of Indians drink chai. This is a mixture of tea, spices, milk, sugar, and water that has been boiled together in one pot. It is served everywhere in India—in homes, in train stations, in restaurants, and even on street corners. Another Indian drink is *lassi*, a cool concoction of yogurt, ice, and sometimes sugar or fruit.

After eating, many Indians chew *paan* to help their digestion. Paan is a mixture of betel nuts, spices, and lime paste wrapped in an edible betel leaf. When people chew it, it

makes their saliva red so that when they spit, they leave little
red splotches on the ground.

Preparing paan

Indians usually eat their food off metal plates or fresh
banana leaves. In India, it is polite to eat with the tips of the
fingers on the right hand. In public eating places, there are
usually sinks or water jugs where people wash their hands
before and after eating. Indians say that eating with your
hands is the only way to get the feel of your food and truly be
able to appreciate it.

Timeline

Indian History

The Indus Valley civilization flourishes at Mohenjo-Daro and Harappa.	2500 B.C.
Aryans arrive in India.	1500
The Buddha is born.	563
Alexander the Great invades India.	327
Emperor Ashoka converts to Buddhism.	262
Chandragupta I founds the Gupta Empire.	A.D. 319
Mohammed of Ghori founds a Muslim empire in northern India.	1192
The Vijayanagar Empire is founded.	1336
Vasco da Gama arrives in India.	1498
The Portuguese conquer Goa.	1510
Babur founds the Mughal Empire.	1526
Queen Elizabeth I charters the East India Company.	1600
France establishes a trading post at Pondicherry.	1672

World History

2500 B.C.	Egyptians build the Pyramids and Sphinx in Giza.
A.D. 313	The Roman emperor Constantine recognizes Christianity.
610	The prophet Muhammad begins preaching a new religion called Islam.
1054	The Eastern (Orthodox) and Western (Roman) Churches break apart.
1066	William the Conqueror defeats the English in the Battle of Hastings.
1095	Pope Urban II proclaims the First Crusade.
1215	King John seals the Magna Carta.
1300s	The Renaissance begins in Italy.
1347	The Black Death sweeps through Europe.
1453	Ottoman Turks capture Constantinople, conquering the Byzantine Empire.
1492	Columbus arrives in North America.
1500s	The Reformation leads to the birth of Protestantism.
1776	The Declaration of Independence is signed.
1789	The French Revolution begins.

Indian History

The Sepoy Mutiny breaks out.	1857
Queen Victoria is named Empress of India.	1877
The India National Congress is founded.	1885
The All-India Muslim League is founded.	1906
British Parliament issues a declaration for eventual self-rule in India.	1917
Indians are killed and wounded in the Amritsar Massacre.	1919
Mahatma Gandhi leads the Salt March.	1930
The British pass the Government of India Act.	1935
India wins independence from Great Britain; Partition divides it into two nations, India and Pakistan; India fights its first war with Pakistan over Kashmir.	1947
Mahatma Gandhi is assassinated.	1948
The constitution is adopted.	1950
India fights a war with China.	1962
India fights its second war with Pakistan.	1965
India wins its third war with Pakistan.	1971
The Indian government carries out its first nuclear test.	1974
Indira Gandhi imposes a state of emergency.	1975
Indira Gandhi is assassinated.	1984
The second set of nuclear tests is carried out.	1998
India's population hits 1 billion.	2000

World History

1865	The American Civil War ends.
1914	World War I breaks out.
1917	The Bolshevik Revolution brings Communism to Russia.
1929	Worldwide economic depression begins.
1939	World War II begins, following the German invasion of Poland.
1945	World War II ends.
1957	The Vietnam War starts.
1969	Humans land on the moon.
1975	The Vietnam War ends.
1979	Soviet Union invades Afghanistan.
1983	Drought and famine in Africa.
1989	The Berlin Wall is torn down as Communism crumbles in Eastern Europe.
1991	Soviet Union breaks into separate states.
1992	Bill Clinton is elected U.S. president.
2000	George W. Bush is elected U.S. president.

Fast Facts

Official name: Republic of India

Capital: New Delhi

Gateway of India

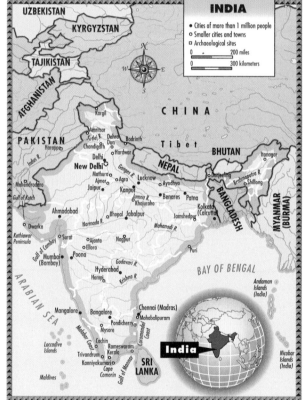

Country's flag

Himalaya Mountains

Official languages:	Assamese, Bengali, Gujarati, Hindi, Kannada, Kashmiri, Malayalam, Marathi, Oriya, Punjabi, Sanskrit, Sindhi, Tamil, Telugu, Urdu
Official religions:	None
Founding date:	Independence from Great Britain, 1947
National anthem:	"*Jana-gana-mana,*" written by Rabindranath Tagore
Government:	Federal Republic
Chief of state:	President
Head of government:	Prime minister
Area:	1,269,438 square miles (3,287,590 sq km)
Latitude and longitude of geographic center:	About 20° north, about 77° east
Bordering countries:	Nepal, Tibet (China), Bhutan, Myanmar, Bangladesh, Pakistan
Highest elevation:	Kanchenjunga, 28,208 feet (8,598 m)
Lowest elevation:	Sea level
Average temperature extremes:	113°F (45° C) in summer; –4°F (–20°C) in winter

Average annual rainfall:

Delhi	25 inches (64 cm)
Mumbai	71 inches (180 cm)
Shillong Plateau	450 inches (1,143 cm)
Thar Desert	Less than 10 inches (25 cm)

National population: 1,014,003,817 (2000 est.)

India Gate

Population of largest cities (2000 est.):

Mumbai	15 million
Kolkata	12 million
Delhi	11.3 million
Chennai	5.9 million
Bangalore	5.2 million

Famous landmarks:

- ▶ *Kanchenjunga*, world's second-tallest mountain (Sikkim)
- ▶ *Raj Path and government buildings* (New Delhi)
- ▶ *Taj Mahal* (Agra)
- ▶ *Gateway of India* (Mumbai)
- ▶ *Red Fort* (Old Delhi)
- ▶ *Victoria Memorial* (Kolkata)

Industry: Agriculture contributes 25 percent of India's gross domestic product (GDP) and employs about 65 percent of the nation's population. Some of the most important crops are sugarcane, rice, wheat, cotton, and tea. India's industries include the mining of metals and natural resources and the manufacturing of products such as textiles, machinery, chemicals, and processed food. Its industries contribute 30 percent of India's GDP. The services sector contributes 45 percent of the GDP and includes transportation, communications, and tourism.

Currency: India's basic unit of currency is the rupee, which is divided into 100 paise. In mid-2001, U.S.$1 = 47.2 rupees

System of weights and measures: Metric system

Literacy (1995 est.): 52 percent

Currency

Young woman

Indira Gandhi

Common Hindi words and phrases:

Namaste or *namaskar*	Hello/Good-bye
Phir milege.	See you soon.
Dhanyavad or *Shukriya.*	Thank you.
Koi bat nahi.	You're welcome.
Kshama kijiye	Sorry
Kripaya	Please
Ji ha	Yes
Ji nahi	No
Ap kaisi/e hai?	How are you?
Bas ap sunaiye	Fine, and you?
Ek minat rukiye	Just a minute
Shubh kamnae!	Good luck!
Thik hai.	It's okay.
Mera ma. . . hai	My name is. . . .
Zara suniye.	Excuse me.

Famous Indians:

Dr. B. R. Ambedkar (1891–1956)
Law minister and social leader

Emperor Ashoka (291–232 B.C.)
Political and religious leader

Indira Gandhi (1917–1984)
Prime minister

Mohandas K. "Mahatma" Gandhi (1869–1948)
Political and spiritual leader

Mohammed Ali Jinnah (1876–1948)
Political leader and first governor-general of Pakistan

Jawaharlal Nehru (1889–1964)
Prime minister

Satyajit Ray (1921–1992)
Filmmaker

Ravi Shankar (1920–)
Musician and composer

Siddhartha Gautama (563–483 B.C.)
Founder of Buddhism

Rabindranath Tagore (1861–1941)
Poet and novelist

To Find Out More

Nonfiction

▶ Brace, Steve. *India*. Portsmouth, N.H.: Heineman Library, 1999.

▶ Cumming, David. *The Ganges Delta and Its People*. Stamford, Conn.: Thomson Learning, 1994.

▶ Schmidt, Jeremy. *In the Village of the Elephants*. New York: Walker and Company, 1994.

▶ Srinivasan, Radhika and Rodbika. *India*. Tarrytown, N.Y.: Benchmark Books, 1994.

Fiction

▶ Dalal-Clayton, Diksha. *The Adventures of Young Krishna: The Blue God of India*. New York: Oxford University Press, 1997.

▶ Ernst, Judith. *The Golden Goose King: A Tale Told by the Buddha*. Chapel Hill, N.C.: Parvardigar Press, 1995.

▶ Ramanujan, A. K. *Folktales from India: A Selection of Oral Tales from Twenty-Two Languages*. New York: Pantheon Books, 1994.

Videos

▶ *Emerging Powers: India*. New Video Group, 1996.

▶ *India: Land of Spirit and Mystique*. Ivn Entertainment, 1988.

▶ *India: Splendor of Rajasthan*. Choices, Inc., 2000.

▶ *Our Musical Heritage – Music of India*. Timeless Video Inc., 1994.

▶ *A Passage to India*. Columbia/Tristar Studios, 1984 (video release, 1991). The story of the conflicts between Indians and British colonialists, based on a novel by E. M. Forster.

▶ *Pather Panchali*. Columbia/Tristar Studios, 1955 (video release, 1996). The story of a family's struggles in a rural Bengali village.

Websites

▶ **Art India**
http://www.webindia.com//
Provides information on Indian traditional painting, contemporary art, architecture, and music. Includes color pictures of Indian art.

▶ **Inda.com Festivals**
http://www.festivals.india.com/festivals/national/republic.html
Describes various national and religious festivals in India—their time, place, reason, and customs.

▶ **Images of India**
http://www.geocities.com/Tokyo/Shrine/4287/
Provides details of Hindu epics, Indian classical music and dance, Indian languages, and social customs.

▶ **Indian Parliament**
http://alfa.nic.in/
Profiles of Indian government leaders, a replica of the constitution, and descriptions of bill policies, political debates, and various political publications.

▶ **World Factbook: India**
http://www.odci.gov/cia/publications/factbook/in.html
Provides information on India's geography, people, government, and economy.

Organizations and Embassies

▶ **Embassy of India**
2107 Massachusetts Avenue, NW
Washington, DC 20008
(202) 939-7000

▶ **Consulate General of India**
3 East 64th Street
New York, NY 10021
(212) 774-0600 or (212) 774-0699

▶ **Consulate General of India**
540 Arguello Boulevard
San Francisco, CA 94118
(415) 668-0683 or (415) 668-0662

▶ **Consulate General of India**
NBC Tower
455 North Cityfront Plaza Drive,
Suite #850
Chicago, IL 60611
(312) 595-0405

▶ **Consulate General of India**
Suite 600, 6th Floor,
3 Post Oak Central
1990 Post Oak Boulevard
Houston, TX 77056
(713) 626-2148 or (713) 626-2149

Index

Page numbers in *italics* indicate illustrations.

A

Adivasis, 85, *85*
agriculture, 18, 20, 21, 67, 70–71, 74
Akbar, Emperor (Mughal), 44, *44*
Alexander the Great, 37, *37*
All-India Muslim League, 49
Ambedkar, B. R., 52, *52*
Amritsar Massacre, 50
architecture, 43, 112–113
Aryans, 36
Ashoka, Emperor (Maurya Empire), 38
automobile industry, 72

B

bamboo, 26–27, 28
banyan trees, 26, *26*
Battle of Plassey, 46
Battle of Talikota, 42
Benares, 95
Bengal tigers, 30, *30*
Bharatiya Janata Party (BJP), 63
Bharatpur National Park, 32
billboard advertising, *115*
birch trees, *28*
Bombay. *See* Mumbai
borders, 15–16
Brahma (Hindu god), 83
British India, 46–52
bronze sculpture of Buddha, *39*
Buddhism, 38, 97–99
Buddhist monastery, *91*
Buddhist monks, 99

C

Calcutta. *See* Kolkata
caste system, 36, 52, 98, 124
Cauvery River, *21*
Chandragupta, 38
Chandragupta I, 39
Chandragupta II, 39
chembarathy flower, 27
Chennai, 19
Chowpatty Beach, 19
Christianity, 40, 103
cinema, 115
climate, 22–23
Clive, Robert, 46
coco palm trees, 27
college students, *122*
communication, 77
Congress Party, 62–63
conservation efforts
    Project Tiger, 30
Corbett National Park, 29
Cornwallis, Lord, 47
cows, 33, *33*
crafts, 113–114
cricket, *105*, 105–106
crops, 70–71
culture
    architecture, 112–113
    caste system, 36, 52, 98, 124
    clothing, 120, *120*
    dance, 107–108, *108*
    death rituals, 123

drama, 109
early influence, 36
education, 121–122
family life, 118
food, 124–127
housing, 123–124
lifestyle, 9–13, 117–118
literature, 109–111
local crafts, 113–114
marriage and weddings, 80, *119*,
119–121
movies, 115
music, 106–107
painting and sculpture, 111–112
sports and hobbies, 105, *105*
currency, 69, *69*
cyclones, 23

D

dance, 107–108
Darius, King of Persia, 37
death rituals, 123
Deccan Plateau, 20–21
dharma, 94, 95
dialects. *See* languages
doing laundry, *10*
drama, 109
Dravidians, 35, 36
droughts, 23

E

Eastern Ghats, 20
East India Company, 45, 46–47, 48
economy, 54, 67–69
and industry, 72
and mining/energy, 73–75
and tourism, 75
education, 121–122
elections
rally gathering, *63*
voter casting ballot, *57*

electronics industry, 72, *72*
elephants, 30
Elizabeth I, Queen of England, 45
empires
Gupta, 39
Maurya, 38
Mughal, 43–44, 112–113
in the South, 39–40, 42
Vijayanagar, 42, 112
employment, 67–68, 72
energy and mining, 73–75
eucalyptus trees, 26
exports, 67, 68, 72

F

family businesses, 72
family in Varanasi, 80
family life, 118
farming, 18, 20, 21, 67, 70–71, 74
fauna, *24*, 25, 31–32, 33
map of wildlife sanctuaries, *31*
sanctuaries and national parks, 28–30
film industry, 115
fishing, 21
floods, 23
flora, 25–27
coastal, 27
mountainous, 28
food, 124–127
forests, 25–27, 28
France, 46

G

Gama, Vasco da, 41–42, *42*, 44
Gandhi, Indira, *53*, 53–54
Gandhi, Mohandas (Mahatma),
49–52, *51*
Gandhi, Rajiv, 54–55, *55*
Ganges River, 18, *18*, 20, 95, *95*
Gateway of India, 19, *19*
Gautama, Siddhartha, 97–98

geography
    borders, 15–16
    Indo-Gangetic Plain, 18, 20
    landscape, 15
    map, *16*
    mountains, 17–18, 20–21
    Southern Peninsula, 20–21
    Thar Desert, 20
golden langur, *31*
Golden Temple in Amritsar, *54*, 101
government, 57
    constitution, 57
    executive branch, 58–59
    Government of India Act, 50
    independence, 49–52
    judicial branch, 61
    legislative branch, 59–60
    military, 64, *64*
    panchayat, 62, *62*
    Parliament, 59, *59*
    Partition, 51–52
    political parties, 49, 50, 62–63
    state and local, 61–62
Gujarat women, *83*
Gupta Empire, 39
gurdwaras, 101
gurus, 101

H

handicrafts. *See* crafts
health care, 81
Himalaya Mountains, 17, 22
Hinduism, 36, 40, 55, 92–95
Hindu temple, *90*
hockey, 106
Hogenakal Falls, *21*
holy books
    Koran, 96
    Mahabharata, 93
    Vedas, 94
    Zend-Avesta, 102

housing, 67, 88–89, *89*, 123–124
Howrah Bridge, *19*

I

imports, *72*
Independence Movement, 49–52
India Gate, *65*
India National Congress, 49, 50
Indian Museum, 110
Indo-Gangetic Plain, *19*, 20
Industrial Revolution, 48
industry, 67, 68, 72
Indus Valley civilizations, 35–36
instruments, 107
Islam, 40, 55, 96–97

J

Jahan, Shah (Mughal), 43
Jainism, 101–102, *102*
Jama Masjid, *96*
Judaism, 103

K

Kanchenjunga, *17*
karma, 94, 95
Kashmiri shepherds and merchant, *82*
Kaziranga National Park, *29*
Khajuraho temple carvings, *111*
Kolkata, *19*
Koran (holy book), 96

L

Ladakh, *22*
Lakshmi (Hindu goddess), *94*
landscape, 15
languages, 77
    dialects, 86–87
    Dravidian, 86
    English, 87
    Hindi, 86
    Sanskrit, 36, 87

leprosy, 55
lifestyle, 9–13, 117–118
lions, 29
literature, 109–111
livestock, 71
lotus flower, 27, 27

M

Madras. See Chennai
Madras trading post (1640), 45
Mahabharata (holy book), 93
mangrove forests, 27
manufacturing, 72, 74
maps
    Delhi, 65
    exploration routes, 41
    geographical, 16
    geopolitical, 11
    India (sixteenth and seventeenth
        centuries), 43
    major languages, 87
    Maurya Empire, 38
    population density, 81
    resource, 73
    states and territories, 61
    wildlife sanctuaries, 31
marriage and wedding customs, 119,
    119–121
Maurya Empire, 38
medical research, 55
military, 64, 64
minaret, 97
mining and energy, 73–75
Mohammed of Ghori (Muslim ruler), 40
moksha, 95
money, 69, 69
mongoose, 32, 32
monkeys, 31, 31
monsoon, 23
mosques, 97
mother and daughter, 125

mountains, 17–18, 20–21
movies, 115
muezzin, 97
Mughal Empire, 43–44, 112–113
Mumbai, 19
music, 106–107
musician and dancer, 104

N

Nanak, Guru, 99
Narayan, R. K., 110
national holidays, 117
national symbols
    banyan tree, 26, 26
    flag, 58, 58
    Lion of Sarnath, 38
    lotus flower, 27, 27
    peacock, 32, 32
    Royal Bengal tiger, 30, 30
natural disasters, 23
natural resources, 73–75
Nehru, Jawaharlal, 50, 53, 58, 58
Nehru, Motilal, 50
newspapers, 77
nirvana, 98
nuclear missiles, 54, 55
nuclear power, 74–75

O

offshore oil rig, 74

P

paan (food), 126–127, 127
painting and sculpture, 111–112
Partition, 51–52
Parvati (Hindu goddess), 94
peacocks, 32, 32
people
    Adivasis, 85, 85
    Arayan, 36

Dalit, 52, 124
Dravidian, 35, 36, 83, *83*
early civilizations, 35–36
European, 44–52
Greek, 37
Gupta Empire, 39
Hindu, 52, 55
homeless, 68, *68*, 88–89, *89*
Indo-Aryan, 82–83
Indus Valley civilization, 35–36
Maurya Empire, 38
Mongol, 43–44
Mongoloid, 84, *84*
Muslim, 40, 51–52, 55, 96, 96–97
Parsis, 103
Persian, 37
Sikh, 55, 99–101, *100*
Vijayanagar Empire, 42
Periyar Wildlife Sanctuary, 29
Permanent Settlement Act, 47
plant life, 25–27
    coastal, 27
    mountainous, 28
plowing a field, *70*
Polo, Marco, 41
population, 19, 65, 79–81
population density, 20, 88
population diversity, 81–85
Porus, King, 37, *37*
prayer flags, *91*
Project Tiger, 30
puja, 95

R
Ramakrishna, Sri, 94, *94*
Rashtrapati Bhavan, 65
Ray, Satyajit, 114, *114*, 115
Red Fort, 43, *43*
reincarnation, 94

relief carving, *35*
religion, 91–92
    Buddhism, 38, 97–99
    Christianity, 40, 103
    Hinduism, 36, 40, 55, 92–95
    Islam, 40, 55, 96–97
    Jainism, 101–102, *102*
    Judaism, 103
    Sikhism, 55, 99–101
    Zoroastrianism, 102–103
rhinoceroses, 30
rice fields, *18*
rivers and canals, *14*, 17, 18, 20, 21
rubber trees, *25*, 27

S
Salt March, 51
sal trees, 27
sand dunes, *15*
Sarasvati (Hindu goddess), 94
Sasan Gir Lion Sanctuary, 29
schoolchildren, *10*, *122*
schoolgirls, *79*
Secretariat building, 56
Sepoy Mutiny, 48, *48*
Shankar, Ravi, 107, *107*
Sharma, Rakesh, 55
Shastri, Lal Bahadur, 53
Shiva (Hindu god), 93, *93*, 95
Siddhartha Gautama, 97–98
Sikhism, 55, 99–101, *100*
Singh, Gobind, Guru, 100
sitar, 107, *107*
Southern Peninsula, 20–21
spiritual salvation, 95
sports and hobbies, 105–106
statue of Harrapa culture, *35*
Sundarbans Wildlife Sanctuary, 29
swadeshi movement, 50

T

Tagore, Rabindranath, 110, *110*
Taj Mahal, 43, *113*
tea, 28
teak trees, 25
tea taster, *71*
telephone system, 77
television, 77
textile industry, 72
textiles, handmade, 113–114
Thar Desert, 20
tigers, 30, *30*
timeline, historical, 128–129
tourism, 75, *75*
trade, 37, 44–45
transportation, 76
    airlines, 77
    animals, 33
    buses, 76
    railroads, 76
    subway, 77
    train station, *76*
    tricycle cart, 66

V

Varanasi, 95
Vardhamana, 101

Vedas (holy books), 93
Vijayanagar Empire, 42, 112
village-based industries, 72.
    See also crafts
village women drawing water, 8
Vindhya Range, 20
Vishnu (Hindu god), 93

W

water buffalo, *13*
weddings. *See* marriage and
    wedding customs
Western Ghats, 20, *20*
wild asses, *24*, 30
wildlife, *24*, 25, 31–32, 33
    map of sanctuaries, *31*
    sanctuaries and national parks,
        28–30, 32
woman shapes dung for fuel, 9
women carrying sheaves of wheat, *70*
wood carving, *114*

Z

Zarathustra, 102
Zend-Avesta (holy book), 102
Zoroastrianism, 102–103

Meet the Author

Erin Pembrey Swan started traveling at the age of nineteen, when she visited Greece for the first time. Since then, she has traveled through most of the United States, parts of Canada and Mexico, several countries in Europe, Egypt, and Nepal. She has spent a considerable amount of time in India, traveling through the country and working for volunteer organizations including Mother Teresa's Missionaries of Charity.

"India is the most interesting country I have ever visited. It seems very confusing and complicated at first, but it is really a very organized society. In this book, I have combined what I learned there with information that I found in my research. Some of my favorite resources are personal nonfiction accounts, government publications, and novels and short stories written by Indian authors.

"I also read history books, religious texts, and even tourist guides. The Internet was one of my best sources for information about India. I found current news stories, cricket match results, examples of Indian art, and even detailed maps of Indian cities. If I ever got stuck for a piece of information, I always turned to the Internet for help."

Erin grew up in New York, both in Manhattan and farther upstate. This book is her seventh for Grolier. Her other publications include children's books about animals around the world, including *Primates: From Howler Monkeys to Humans* and *Land Predators of North America*. She has had a number of poems published in various journals and is currently working to publish her short stories.

Erin has studied literature, animal behavior, and early childhood education at Hampshire College; literature and history at University College Galway; and creative writing, literature, and foreign languages at New School University. She currently lives in Manhattan and is already planning more trips to foreign countries, including a return to India.

Photo Credits

AKG London: 34, 35, 113 (Jean-Louis Nou), 44, 51 top, 58 bottom, 110

AllSport USA/Getty Images/Mike Hewitt: 105

Ann Jastrab: 80, 111

Archive Photos/Getty Images/ Hulton Getty Archive: 42

BBC Natural History Unit: 32 bottom (Bernard Castelein), 32 top (Ashok Jain), 30 (E.A. Kuttapan), 20 (Ian Lockwood), 24, 31 bottom (Anup Shah)

Bridgeman Art Library International Ltd., London/New York: 39 (National Museum of India, New Delhi), 45 (Private Collection)

Corbis-Bettmann: 92 (Lindsay Hebberd), 100 (Earl & Nazima Kowall), 52 bottom, 94

David R. Frazier: 65 bottom, 132 top

Dinodia Picture Agency: 66 (M. Amirtham), 56 (Viren Desai), 74 (Pradip Gupta), 18 bottom (S. Mehta), 53, 133 bottom (Firoze Mistry), 70 top (Mahendra Patil), 7 top, 43 bottom (J.R. Raul), 114 bottom (T.S. Satyan), 69, 132 bottom (Rajesh H. Sharma), 108, 122 bottom (Ravi Shekhar), 76 (Rajesh Vora), 10 bottom, 28, 54, 62, 63, 78, 99, 109, 115, 127

Erin Swan: 91

Halley Gatenby: 68, 82

International Stock Photo: 22, 131 bottom (Merrill Images), 2 (Charles Westerman)

Liaison Agency, Inc./Getty Images/ Pablo Bartholomew: 55, 57, 59, 64

MapQuest.com, Inc.: 58 top, 131 top

Mary Evans Picture Library: 37, 40, 48, 51 bottom, 52 top

Panos Pictures: 89 (Peter Barker), 9 (Trygve Bolstad), 15 (J.C. Callow), 83 top, 133 top (Neil Cooper), 71 (Jean-Leo Dugast), 125 (Nancy Durrell-Tickema), 7 bottom, 83 bottom, 103 (Daniel O'Leary), 33 (Paul Quayle), 67 (Paul Smith), 123 (Sean Sprague), 122 top (Liba Taylor), 90, 117 (Ray Wood)

Photo Researchers, NY: 27 (Dr. Jeremy Burgess/SPL), 25 (Joyce Photographics), 26 (Gunter Kiepke/Naturbild/ OKAPIA), 29 (Mandal Ranjit);

Stone/Getty Images: 104 (Ben Edwards), 19, 130 left (Chris Haigh), cover, 6 (Hilarie Kavanagh)

The Image Works: 85 (R.A. Acharya/ DPA), 21, 116 (M. Amirtham/DPA), 114 top, 70 bottom, 72, 79, 120 (DPA), 96 (DPA/NSR), 17, 84 (Macduff Everton), 10 top, 86 (Margot Granitsas), 8 (M. Justice), 119 (N. Naoroji/DPA), 18 top (Ajit Parekh/DPA), 102 (Christine Pemberton), 95 (L. Rorke), 93, 107 (Topham), 118 (Alison Wright)

Viesti Collection, Inc./Tettoni, Cassio & Associates/Photobank: 14

Visuals Unlimited/Joe McDonald: 13

Wolfgang Kaehler: 75

Maps by Joe LeMonnier.